Gold Stars®

200 Maths and English Activities

Ages 4-5

Written by
David and Penny Glover
Betty Root

PaRRagon

Bath · New York · Singapore · Hong Kong · Cologne · Delhi · Melbourne

Helping your child

- Do talk about what's on the page. Let your child know that you are sharing the activities.

- Explain what has to be done on each page, and help with any recording such as colouring and joining up.

- Do not become anxious if your child finds any of the activities too difficult. Young children develop and learn at different rates.

- Let your child do as much or as little as he or she wishes. Do leave a page that seems too difficult and return to it later.

- It is important to work through the pages in the right order because the activities do get progressively more difficult.

- Always give your child lots of encouragement and praise.

- Remember that the gold stars and badges are a reward for effort as well as for achievement.

First published by Parragon in 2007
Parragon
Queen Street House
4 Queen Street
Bath BA1 1HE, UK

Copyright © Parragon Books Ltd 2007

ISBN 978-1-4054-9687-2

Printed in Malaysia

Contents

Conte...

Contents

Contents

Little

Look at the pictures.
Put a tick by the things that are little.

Note for parent: Describing and comparing things starts
your child's mathematical development.

Big

Draw a ring around the things that are big.

Pigs

Can you see where the wolf is hiding?
Draw lines to join the pictures to the right words.

Note for parent: Using positional words such as in, on, under, beside and behind develops awareness of space and movement.

In, on, under

Draw a ball on the chair.

Draw a ball under
the table.

Draw a ball in the box.

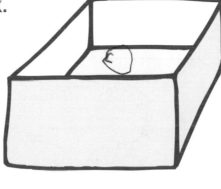

Long and short

Trace the snakes with your finger.
Put a cross by the shortest snake. Say its colour.
Put a tick by the longest snake. Say its colour.

yeevo

greer

red

bloo

Note for parent: Length and height comparisons are the starting
point for measurement.

Short and tall

Look at the giraffes. Put a tick by the shortest giraffe. Put a cross by the tallest giraffe.

Draw lines to join each giraffe to its tree.

Heavy and light

Draw rings around the things that are heavy.

Full or empty?

Look at the pictures. Draw a ring around the things that are empty.

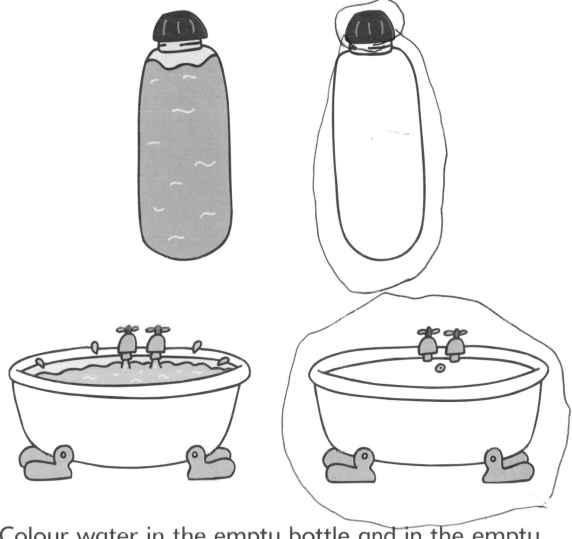

Colour water in the empty bottle and in the empty bath to fill them.

Note for parent: Experiment with filling and emptying plastic containers at bath time.

Three bears

Draw lines to join each bear to the correct chair.

Draw lines to join each bear to the correct bowl.

Note for parent: Sequencing and matching are important number skills.

Draw lines to join each bear to the correct spoon.

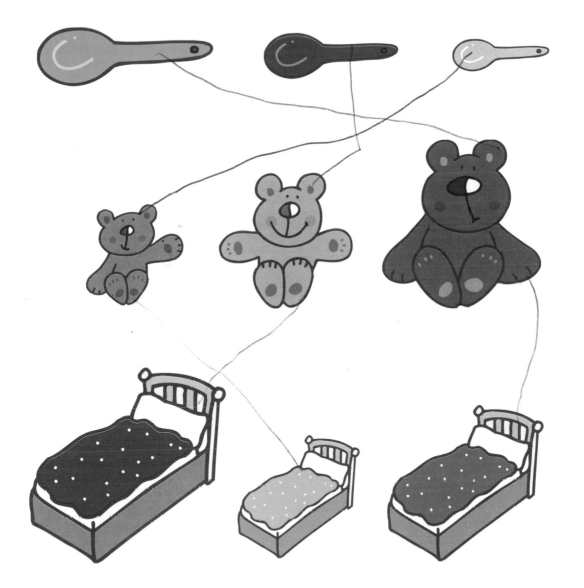

Draw lines to join each bear to the correct bed.

How many?

Draw rings around the correct numbers.

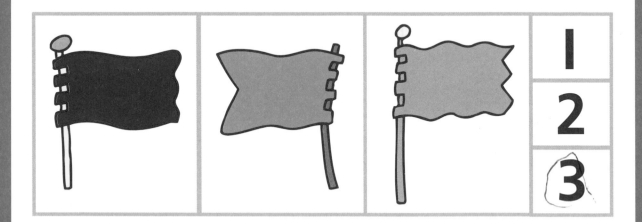

Note for parent: This page shows the numbers 1, 2 and 3 and helps your child with counting.

One, two, three

Draw dots to match the numbers.

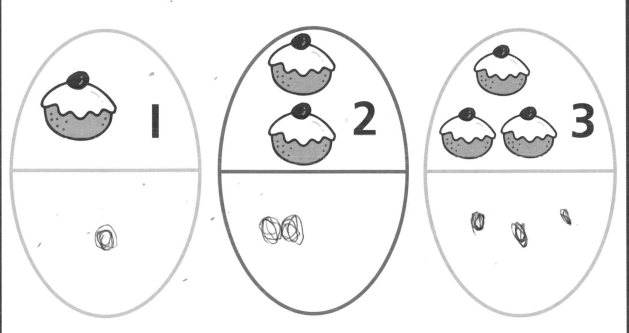

1 2 3

Write in the missing number.

1 2 3

Count the candles

Count the candles on each cake.

How old are you? Draw a ring around the cake you had on your last birthday. Write your age in the box.

Note for parent: Point to real objects or pictures as you practise counting, don't just recite the words.

Count the animals

Count the animals in each set and draw lines to join each set to the correct number.

1
2
3
4
5

Circles

Trace the circles with your finger.
Which circle is the smallest? Which circle is the biggest?

Note for parent: Even though they are different sizes and
colours, all the circles are the same shape.

Find the circles

Look at the picture and find the circles.
Colour them in.

Triangles

Trace the triangle with your finger.

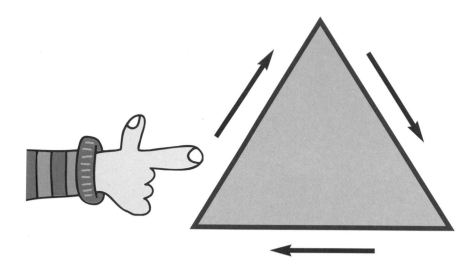

Count the sides – 1, 2, 3. Trace over the dotted lines to complete each triangle.

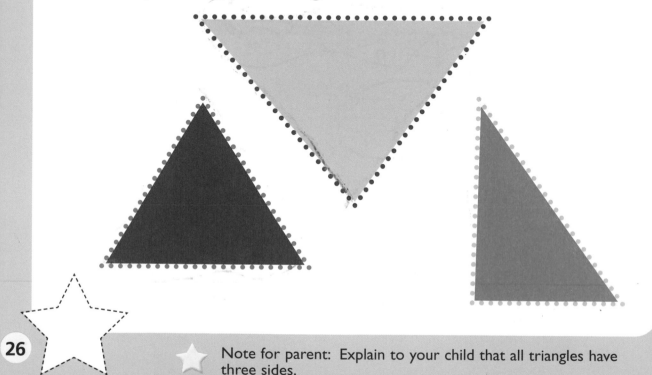

Note for parent: Explain to your child that all triangles have three sides.

Find the triangles

Look at the picture and find the triangles.
Colour them in.

Squares

Trace the square with your finger.
Count the sides – 1, 2, 3, 4.

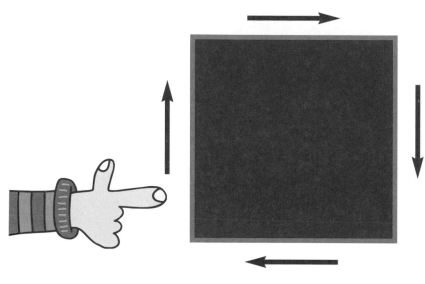

Trace over the dotted lines to finish the squares.
Colour the biggest square red. Colour the smallest
square blue.

Note for parent: Explain to your child that squares have four
equal sides.

Find the squares

Find the squares in this picture.
Colour them in.

Shapes and colours

Look at the pictures. Name each shape and say its colour.

Colour the shapes on these flags to match the ones above.

Note for parent: Knowing about colours and shapes helps children to sort and match.

Match the shapes

Join each object to its shape.

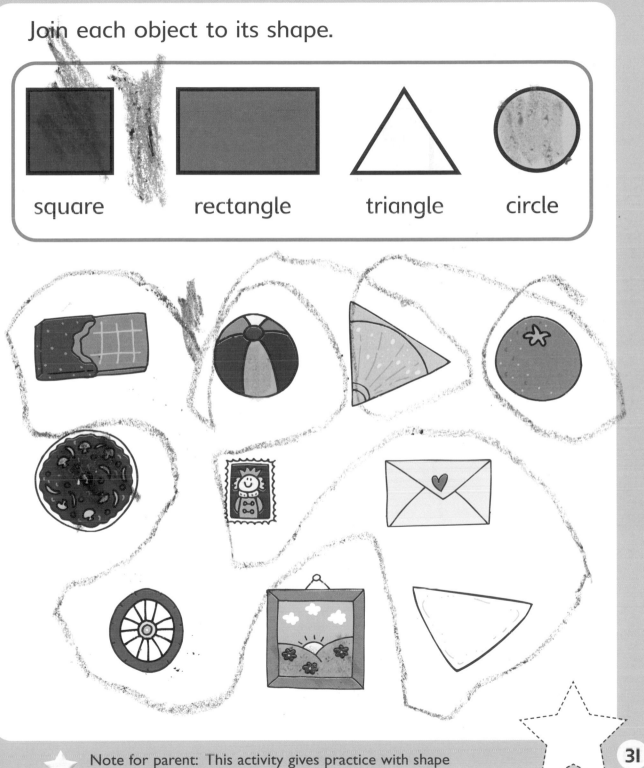

square

rectangle

triangle

circle

Note for parent: This activity gives practice with shape recognition.

Shape fun

Two tractors need new wheels. Draw lines to join the best wheel for each tractor.

Note for parent: This activity gives further practice with shape and colour recognition.

Join the lollies

Draw lines to join the lollies that are the same.

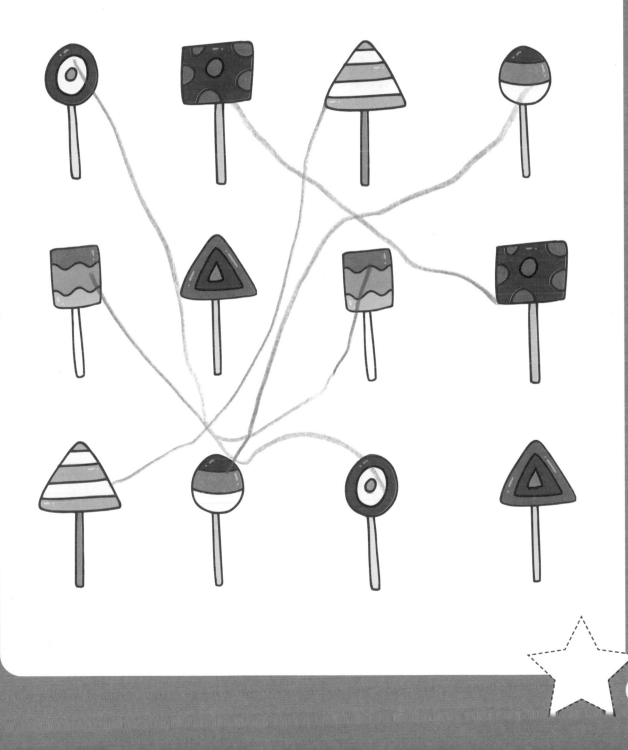

Four, five, six

Draw dots to match the numbers.

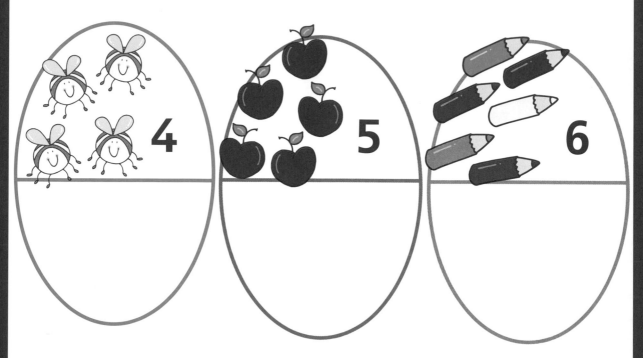

How many candles are on the cake?
Draw a ring around the correct number.

Note for parent: These activities help make the links between the number word you say, the number symbol and a number of things.

Count the bricks

Count the bricks in each set.
Draw lines to join them to the right numbers.

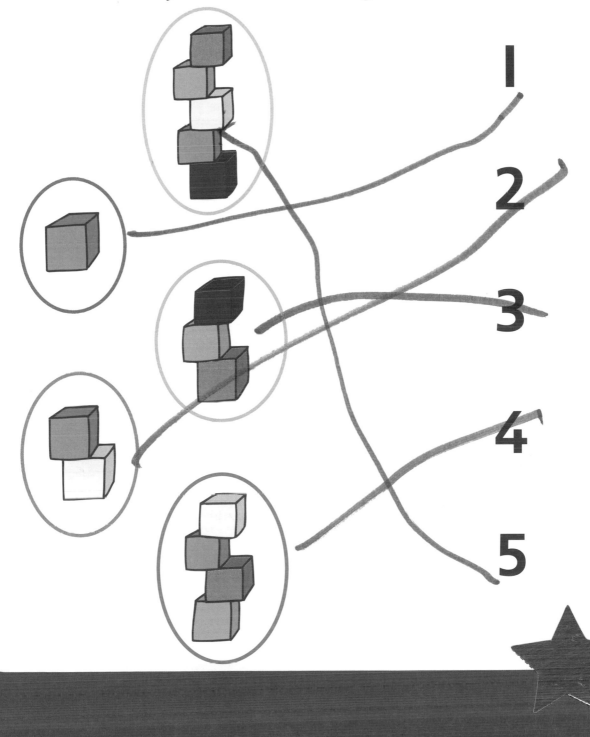

1

2

3

4

5

Up and down

Count up the number stairs.
Count back down again.

Count the ladybirds' spots.
Draw lines to join each ladybird to the right step.

Note for parent: When your child can count five objects confidently, then begin to count to ten. Count down as well as up.

Join the dots

Join the dots in order. What can you see?

 Note for parent: Dot-to-dot drawings develop pencil control, as well as reinforcing counting knowledge.

On the beach

Count these seaside objects. Draw lines to join each set to the correct number.

1

2

3

4

5

6

Note for parent: This activity develops number recognition and counting skills.

Numbers around us

Draw lines to join each car to the correct number.

1 2 3 4 5 6

Note for parent: Numbers are used as labels, to number cars or houses for example, as well as to count 'how many'.

Maze fun

Help the children follow the paths to their houses. Follow each path with your finger.

Note for parent: Encourage your child to concentrate and follow each line accurately.

Seven, eight, nine

Count the red streamers on each kite. Draw the string between each kite and the child with the same number.

Note for parent: This activity provides more counting practice for seven, eight and nine.

Hook a duck

Count the dots on the hooks. Draw a line to join each hook to the correct duck.

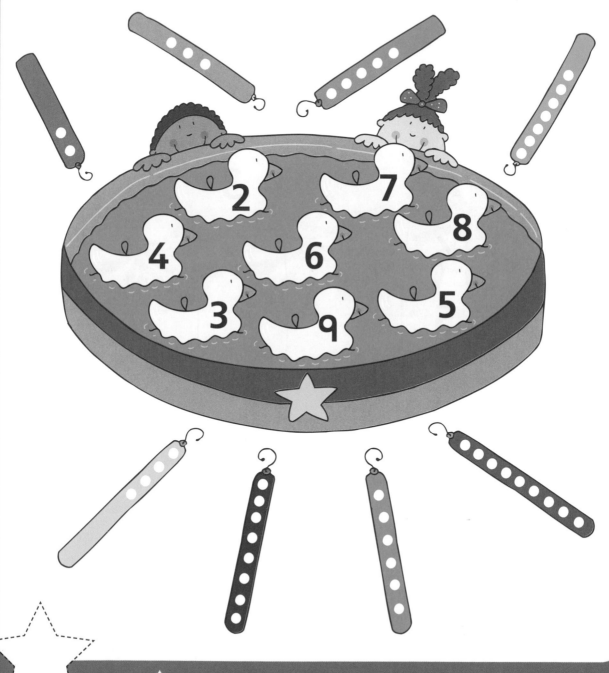

Missing numbers

Trace the dots to write the missing numbers.

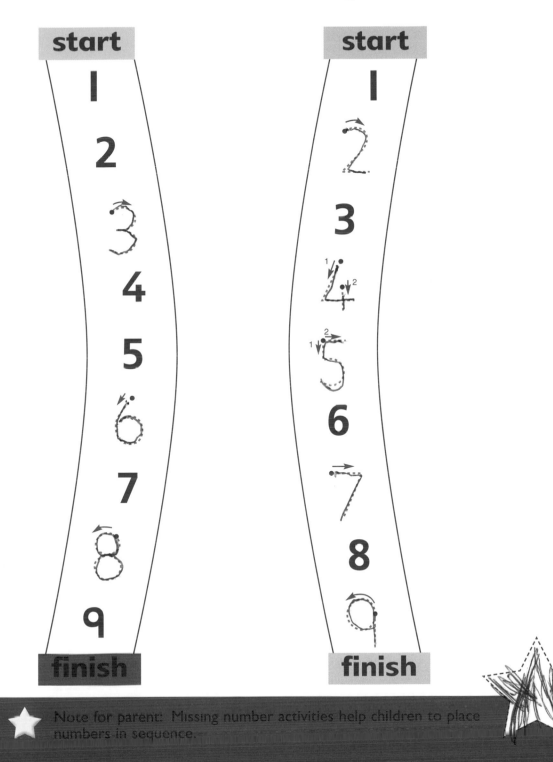

Number snakes

Write the missing numbers on the snakes.

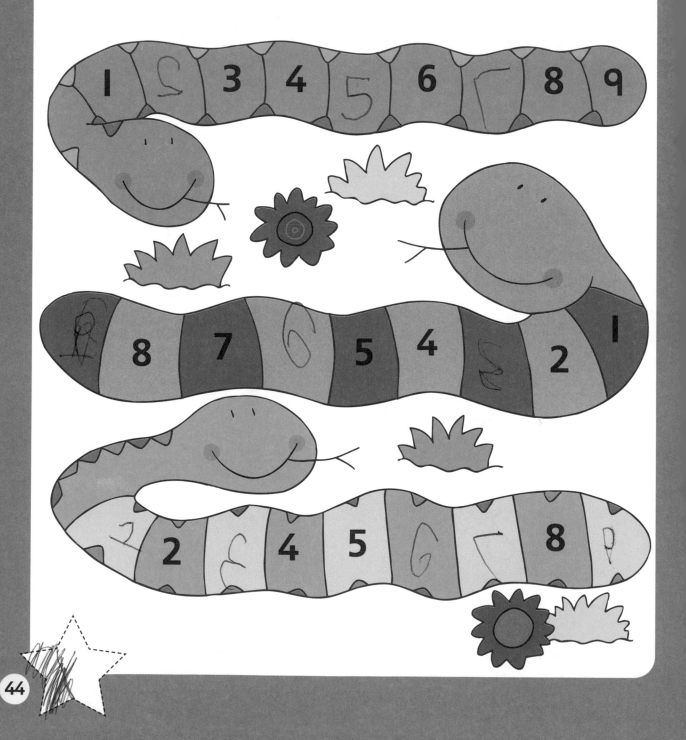

Count to ten

Colour the bottles on the wall. Count the
bottles and circle the right number.

1 2 3 4 5 6 7 8 9 (10)

Count the monster's toes. Circle the
right number.

1
2
3
4
5
6
7
8
9
(10)

Note for parent: Show your child how to count to ten by using
the fingers of both hands.

Climb the ladder

Fill in the missing numbers on the ladder.

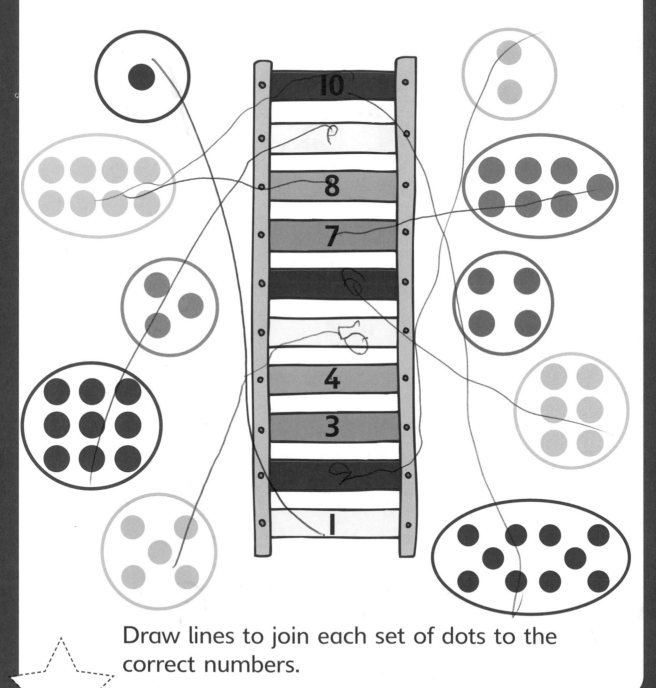

Draw lines to join each set of dots to the correct numbers.

Practice page

Draw a line from each set of balls to the correct number.

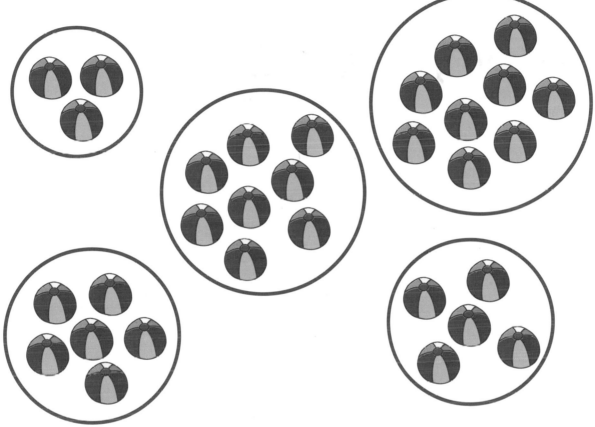

1 2 3 4 5 6 7 8 9 10

Trace the dots to write the numbers up to 10.

1 2 3 4 5 6 7 8 9 10

Making patterns

Trace over the dotted lines. Make a row underneath.

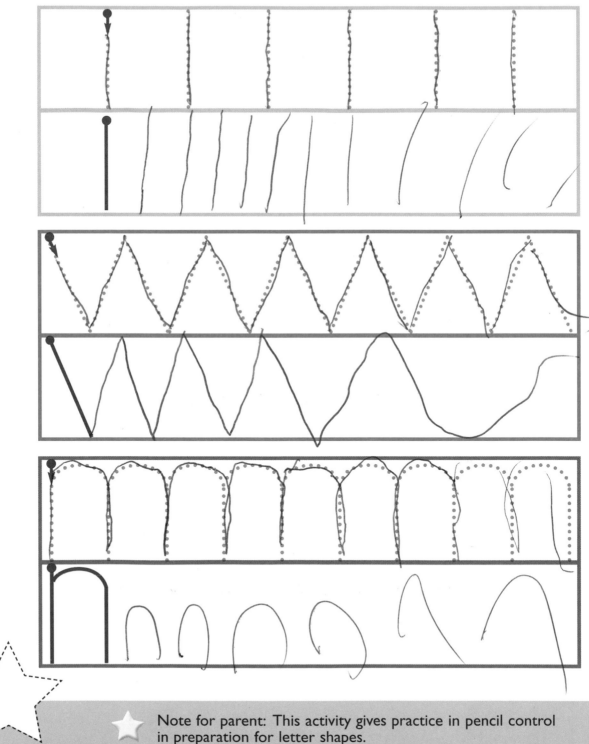

Note for parent: This activity gives practice in pencil control in preparation for letter shapes.

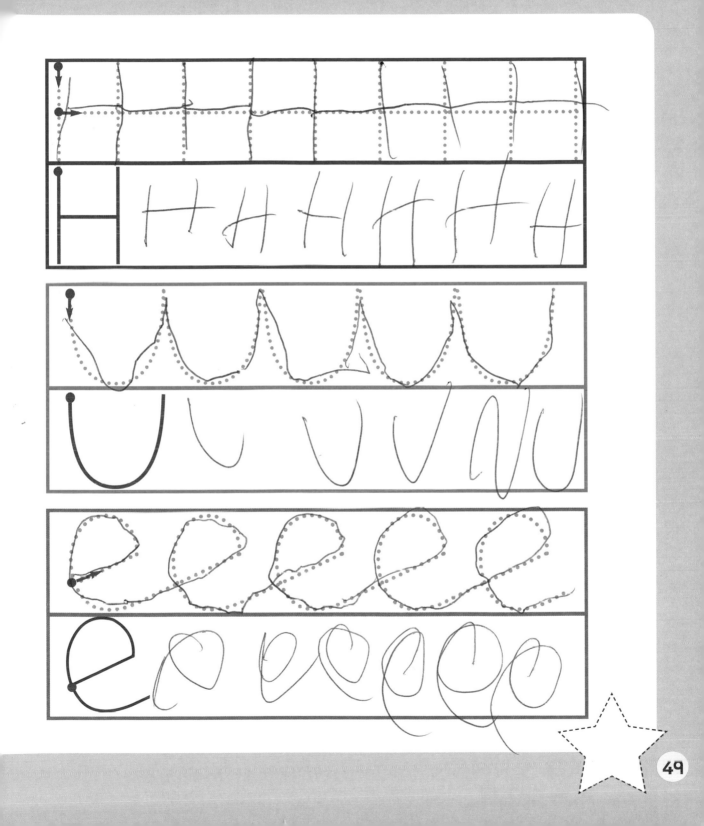

Go together

Start at the red dot. Draw along each path.
Try not to touch the lines.

Note for parent: Keeping between the lines helps pencil control.

Find the balls

Find 5 balls in the picture.
Draw a circle around each one.
Finish the pattern of circles around the picture.
Colour the picture.

 Note for parent: This activity helps children to draw circles.

Shadows

Draw lines to join each picture to its shadow.
Try to make straight lines.
The first one has been done for you.

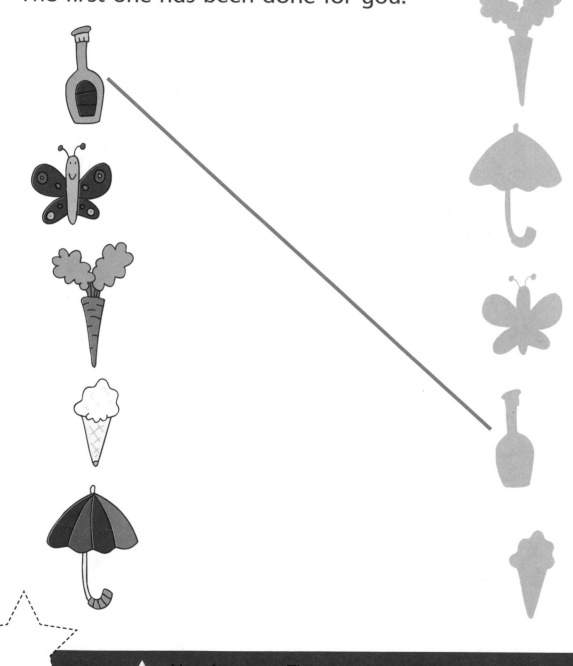

Note for parent: This activity gives children practice in pencil
control for straight and wiggly lines.

Draw lines to join each picture to its shadow.
Try to make wiggly lines.
The first one has been done for you.

A wet day

Draw over the dotted lines to finish the picture.
Colour the picture.

Note for parent: This activity helps children to use a pencil carefully to complete pictures.

What shall I eat?

Start at the red dot. Draw along each path to find out what everyone eats.

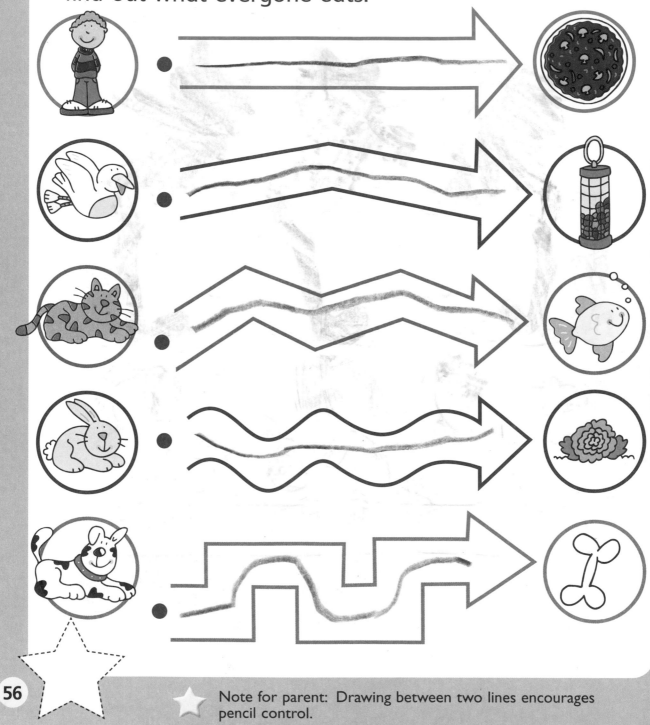

Note for parent: Drawing between two lines encourages pencil control.

Tails

Draw over the dotted lines.
Colour the animals.

Note for parent: Children need to develop a steady hand for good writing.

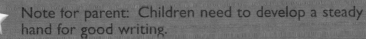

Safari park

Draw over the dotted lines.
Colour the picture.

Note for parent: This activity helps children to use a pencil carefully to complete pictures.

Flying kites

Draw over the dotted lines.
Colour the kites to match the T-shirts.

Note for parent: This gives children practice in
controlling the direction of their pencil.

Trace the pattern

Trace over the dotted lines on each ball.

Note for parent: This activity gives children further practice in pencil control.

Motor mazes

Trace over the dotted lines to find out which car will get to the flag first.

More patterns

Trace over the lines to finish the pictures.

Note for parent: This activity helps children to follow dotted lines to make a pattern.

Making letters 1

Trace over each dotted letter.

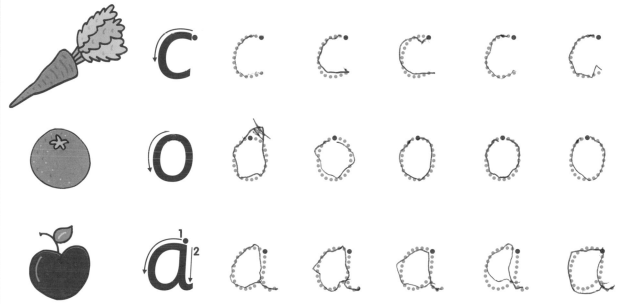

Trace the letters to complete the words.

orange

pple

arrot

Note for parent: This activity helps children to write the letters c, o and a.

63

Making letters 2

Trace over each dotted letter.

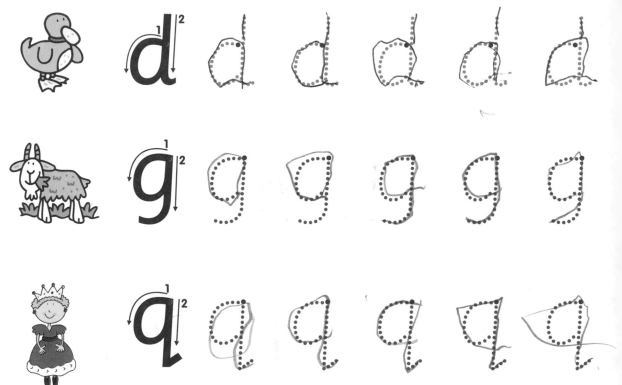

Circle the picture which begins with the letter d.

Note for parent: This activity helps children to write the letters d, g, q, b, h and p.

Trace over each dotted letter.

Say the name of each picture and write its beginning letter.

Making letters 3

Trace over each dotted letter.

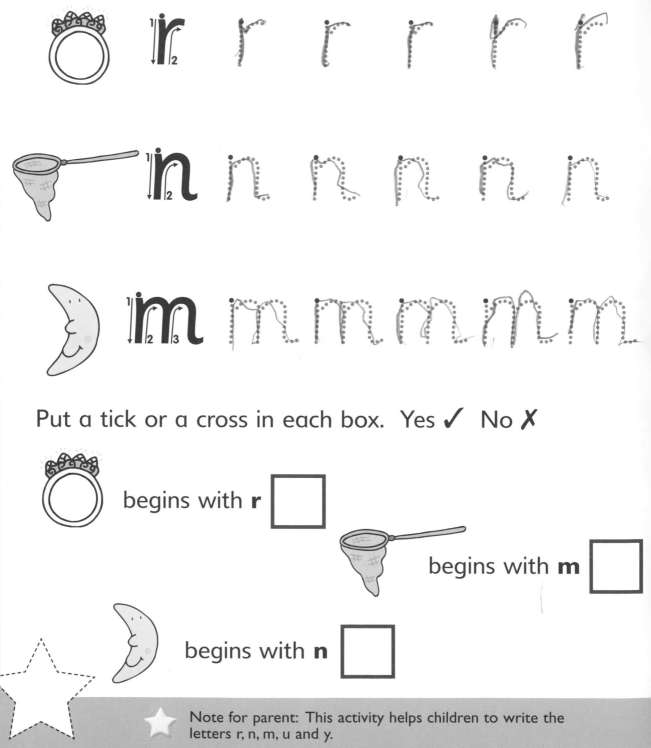

r r r r r r r

n n n n n n n

m m m m m m m

Put a tick or a cross in each box. Yes ✓ No ✗

begins with **r** ☐

begins with **m** ☐

begins with **n** ☐

Note for parent: This activity helps children to write the letters r, n, m, u and y.

Trace over each dotted letter.

Trace the letters to complete the words.

s u n

u mbrella

y ellow

y o - y o

Making letters 4

Trace over the dotted letters.

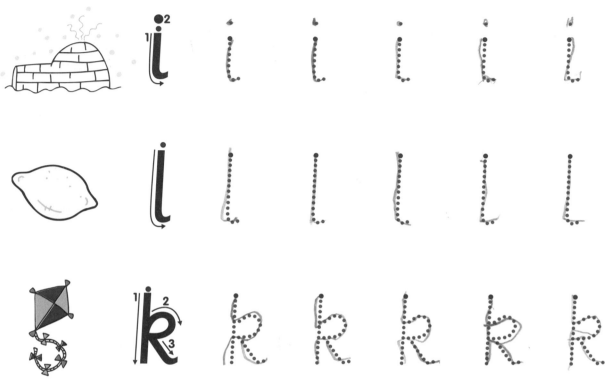

Circle the picture that begins with the letter k.

Note for parent: This activity helps children write the letters
i, l, k, f, j and t.

Trace over the dotted letters.

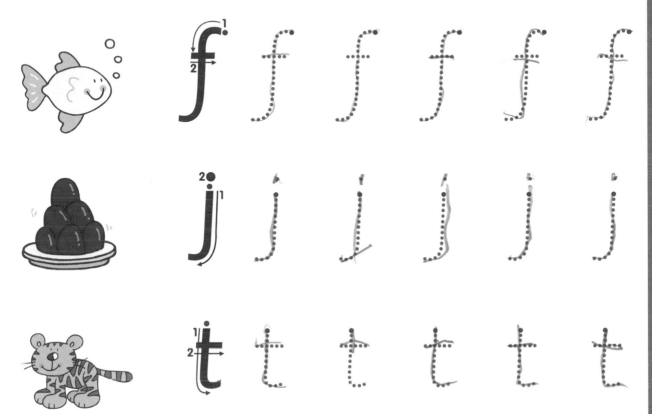

Say the name of each picture.
Cross out the letter which is wrong.

Making letters 5

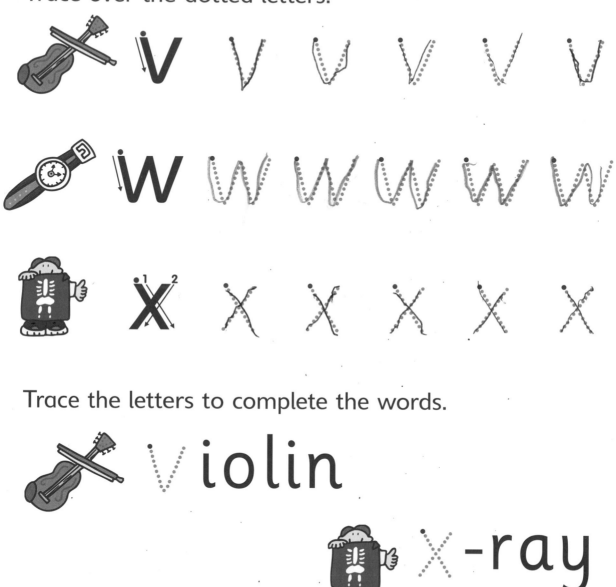

Trace over the dotted letters.

V v v v v v v

W w w w w w w

X x x x x x x

Trace the letters to complete the words.

violin

x-ray

watch

Trace over the dotted letters.

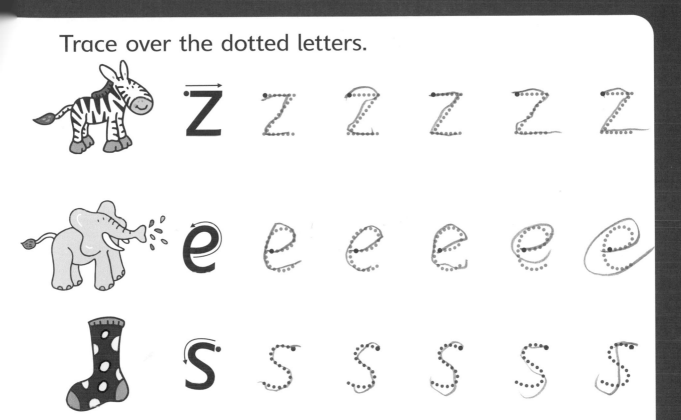

Z z z z z z

e e e e e e

s s s s s s

Draw lines to join the pictures that start in the same way.

Capital letters

Capital letters are used at the beginning of names and other important words.
Trace over the dotted lines to make the letters.

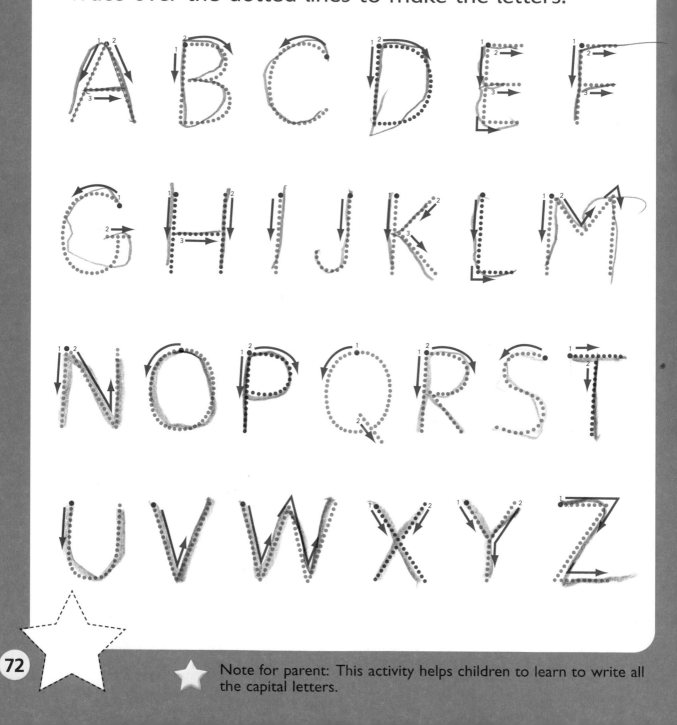

Note for parent: This activity helps children to learn to write all the capital letters.

Writing names

All names begin with a capital letter.
Write the names and colour the pictures.
Draw a picture of yourself and write your name.

Mummy

Daddy

Granny

Note for parent: This activity helps children to learn that names
begin with a capital letter.

Matching letters 1

Trace over the dotted letters.

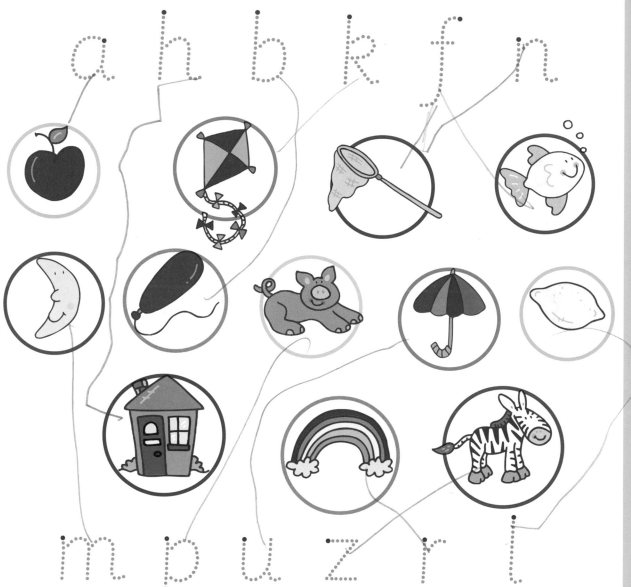

Say the name of each picture.
Draw lines to join each letter to a picture that begins with the same letter.

Note for parent: This activity gives practice in writing and matching letters.

Matching letters 2

Trace over the dotted letters.

c e i u j a s w

Say the name of each picture.
Draw lines to join each letter to a picture that begins with the same letter.

d g o t v x y

First letters

Say the names of these things. Write the first letter of each word under its picture. These are the letters you will need.

b	d	p	q	y	f

Hidden letters

Trace over the dots to write the letters on the shirts.
Draw lines to match the players with the same letters.

Note for parent: This activity helps distinguish letters that are often confused: m and n; u and v. Point and say each letter sound.

A sunny day

Point to the sun, rabbit, butterfly and tree. Trace over the letter shapes on each picture.

Note for parent: Say, "s is for sun," and so on, as your child identifies each shape.

Writing words 1

Trace over the dotted letters to write the words.

pen

cat

mum

dad

dog

box

Writing words 2

Trace over the dotted letters to write the words.

bed

hat

pig

cup

bag

fox

Note for parent: Make sure your child starts writing each letter in the correct place as shown by the bold dot.

Animal parade ✓

Circle the animal in each row that is facing a different way from the others.

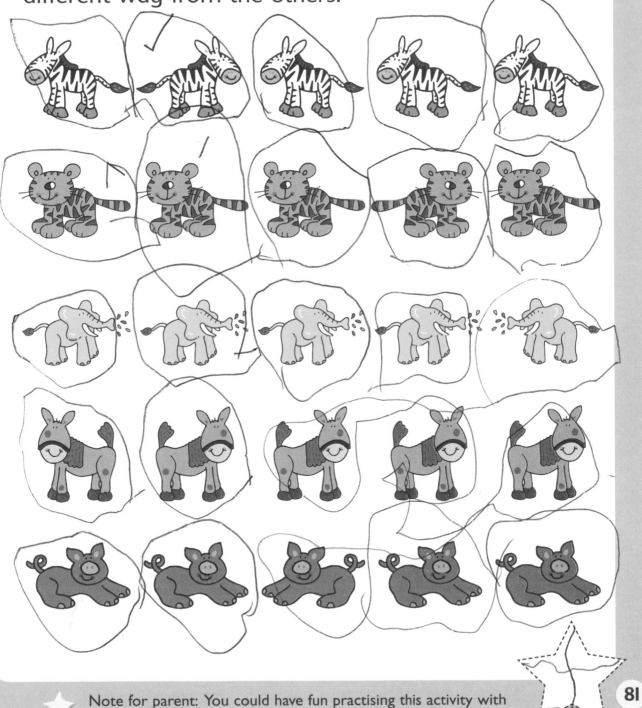

Note for parent: You could have fun practising this activity with a line of toys.

The right way

Circle the odd one out in each row.

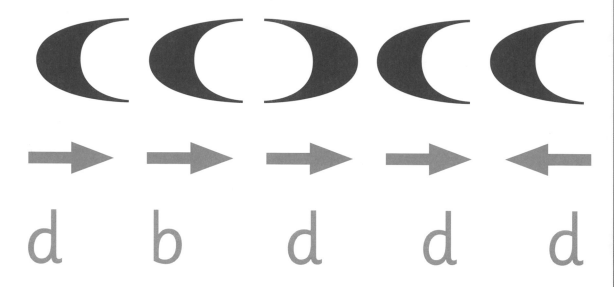

Circle the thing in each row that is upside-down.

82

Note for parent: Learning the correct direction for letter shapes is especially important for left-handers.

I can write

Trace over the dots to write the letters.

Well done! You have written the alphabet.

Note for parent: Writing is hard work for young children. Always praise your child's efforts.

Count to three

How many balloons can you count in each set?

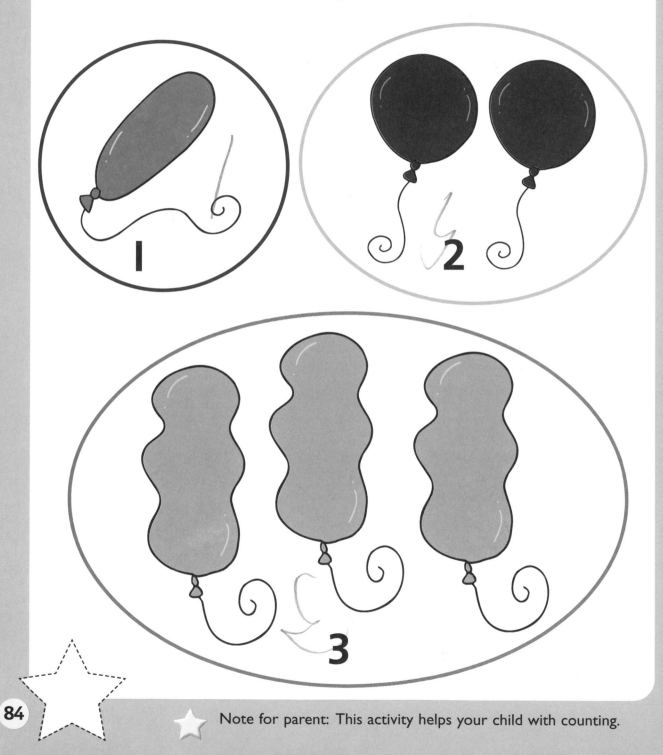

Note for parent: This activity helps your child with counting.

The same

Count the spots on each shirt. Draw lines to join the shirts with the same number of spots.

Note for parent: Identifying numbers that are the same or different prepares your child for adding and subtracting.

Who has more?

Look at the pictures. Put a tick by the person in each row who has more.

Note for parent: This activity gives more practice in counting from one to three.

Another one

Each dog needs a ball. Draw 1 more.

Each child needs a cake. Draw 1 more.

One add one

Point to each picture and count the objects.
Say the numbers out loud.

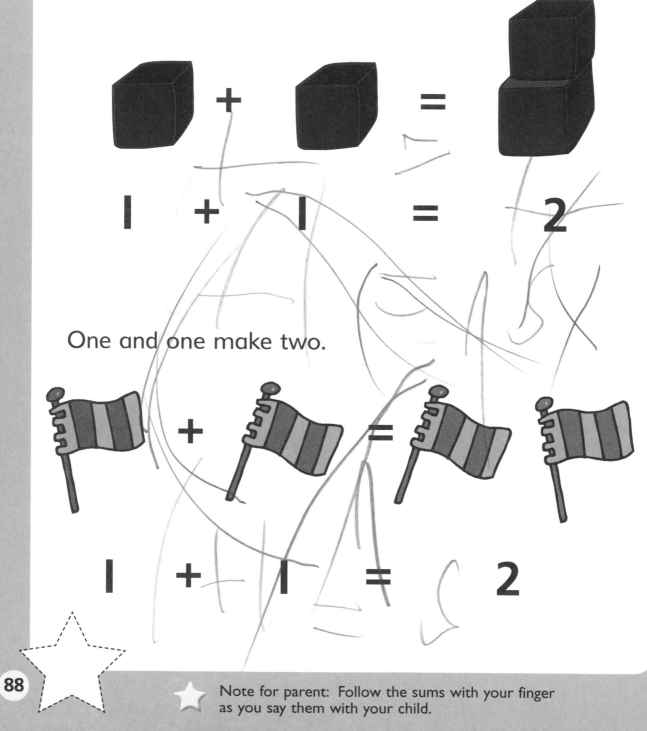

1 + 1 = 2

One and one make two.

1 + 1 = 2

Note for parent: Follow the sums with your finger
as you say them with your child.

Makes two

Write the numbers in the boxes to make the totals.

 +  =

1 + 1 =

1 + 1 =

Two add one

Point to each picture and count the objects.
Say the numbers out loud.

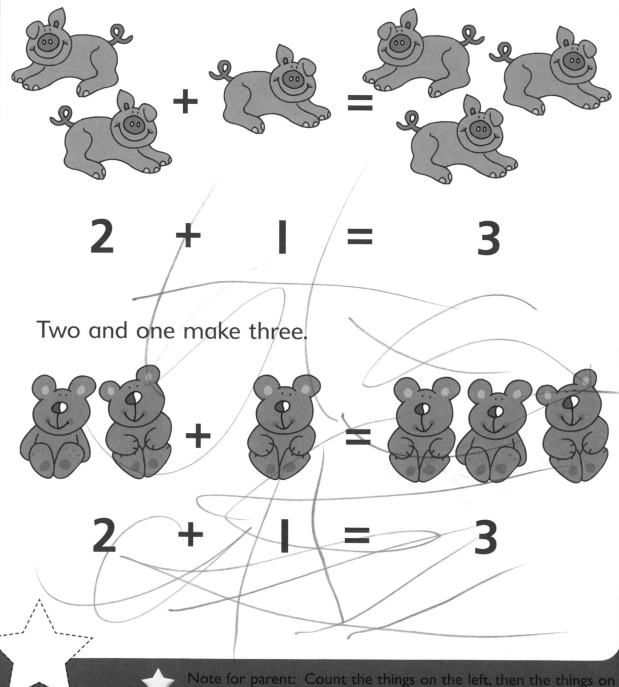

2   +   1   =   3

Two and one make three.

2   +   1   =   3

Makes three

Colour the answers to these sums.

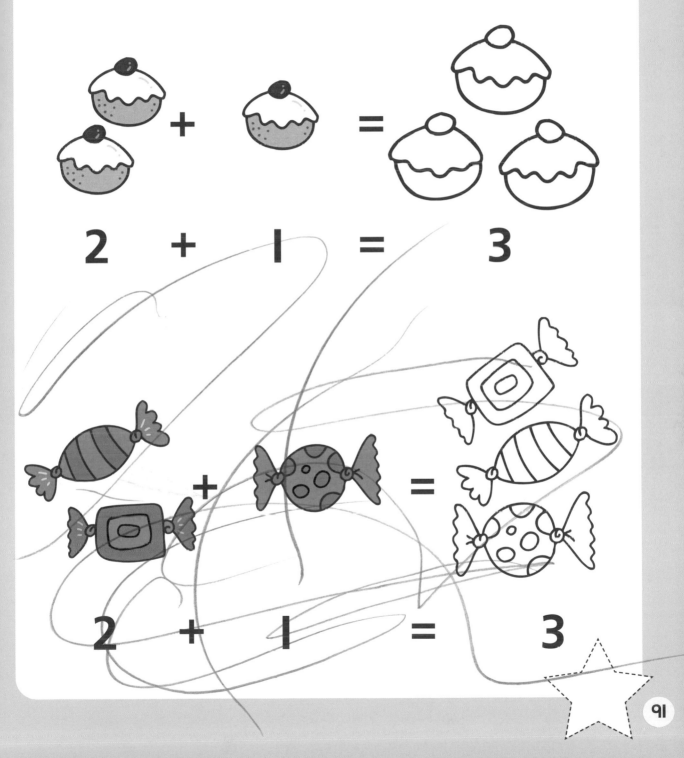

2 + 1 = 3

2 + 1 = 3

Count four and five

Colour four ducks.

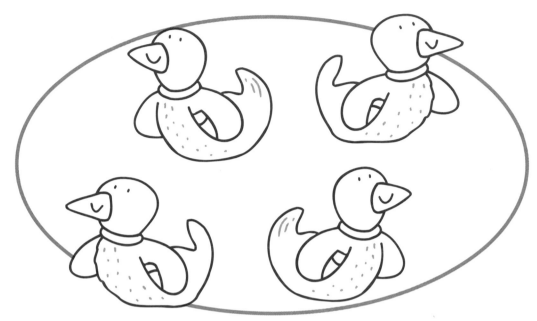

Colour five fish.

Note for parent: Children often find it difficult to count objects that are not arranged in tidy rows.

The same or more?

Join each rabbit to a hole. Are there more rabbits or more holes? Tick the correct box.

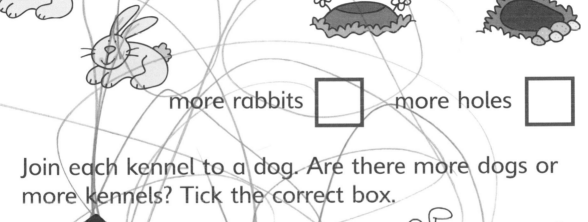

more rabbits ☐   more holes ☐

Join each kennel to a dog. Are there more dogs or more kennels? Tick the correct box.

more kennels ☐   more dogs ☐

Note for parent: Matching objects one by one shows if the numbers are the same or different.

One more

Colour one more flag.

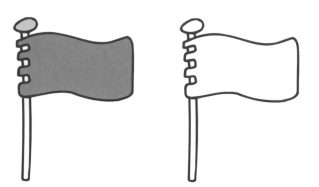

How many flags are there altogether?

Colour one more apple.

How many apples are there altogether?

Note for parent: Use a variety of words to talk about adding — add, and, plus, make, one more, another one, altogether, sum.

Altogether

Colour one more butterfly.

How many butterflies are there altogether?

Colour one more hat.

How many hats are there altogether?

Add one

Point to each picture and count the objects.
Say the numbers out loud.

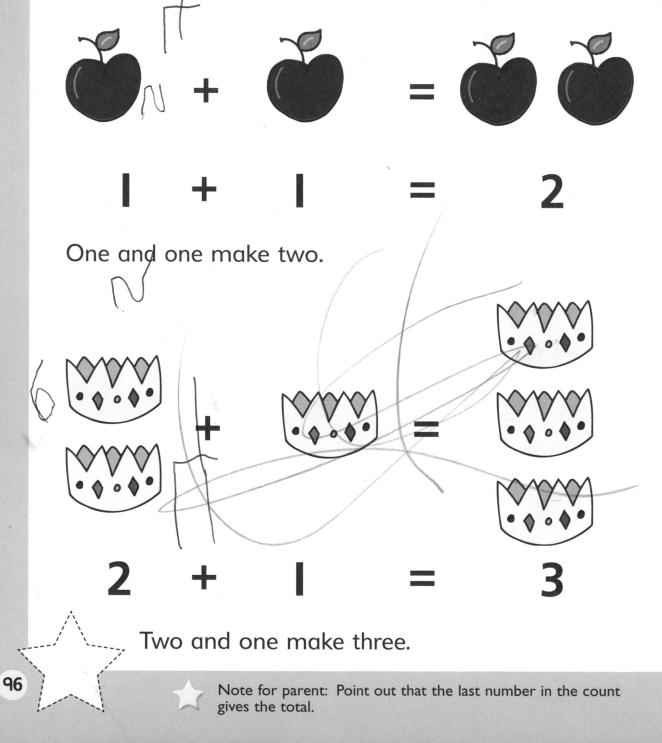

1 + 1 = 2

One and one make two.

2 + 1 = 3

Two and one make three.

Note for parent: Point out that the last number in the count
gives the total.

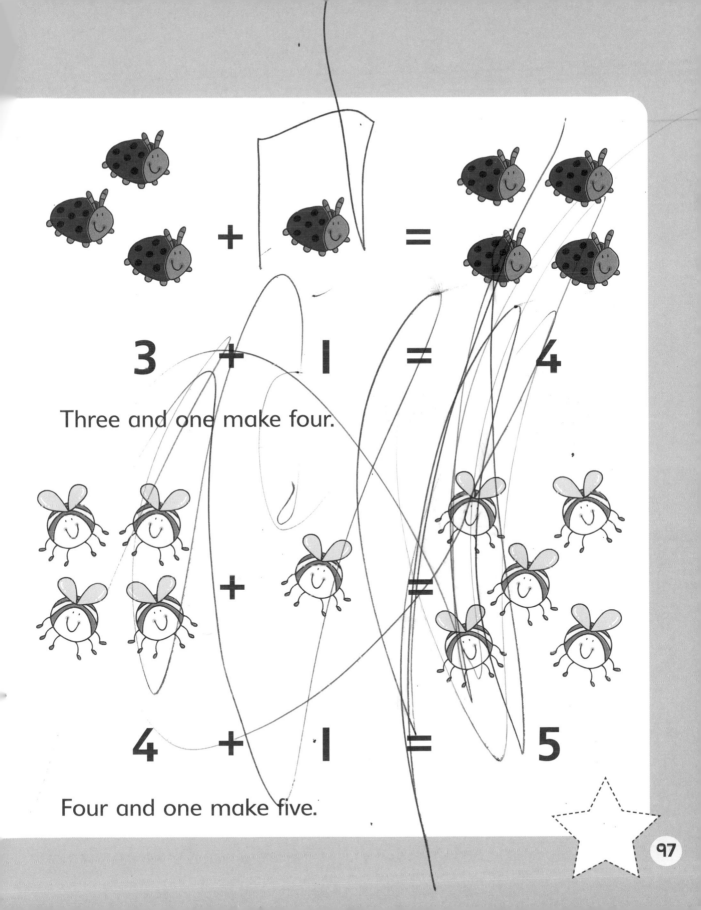

3 + 1 = 4

Three and one make four.

4 + 1 = 5

Four and one make five.

Two more

Colour two more shells.

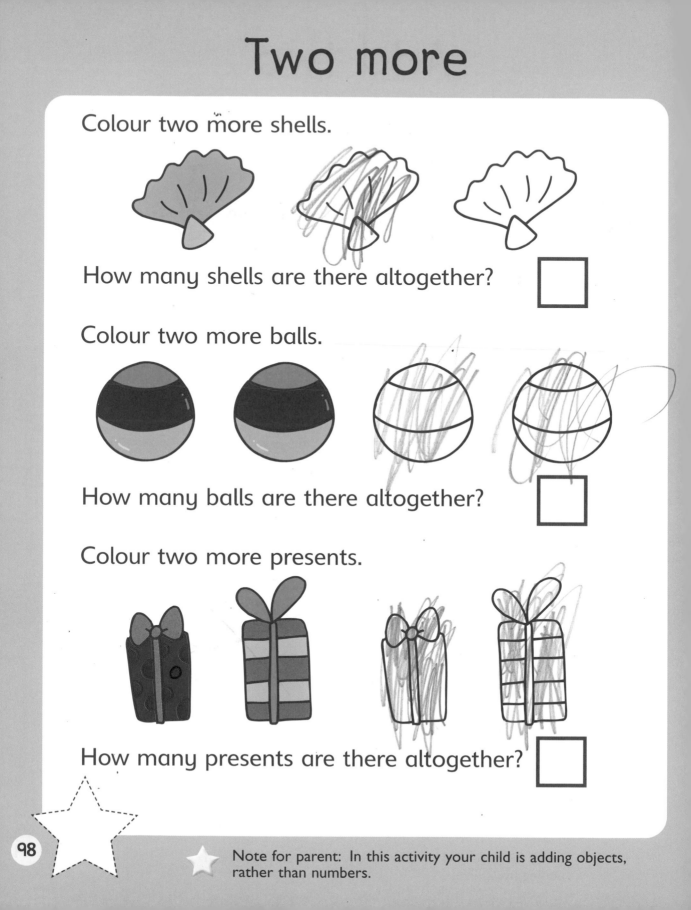

How many shells are there altogether?

Colour two more balls.

How many balls are there altogether?

Colour two more presents.

How many presents are there altogether?

Note for parent: In this activity your child is adding objects, rather than numbers.

Add two

Point to each picture and count the objects.
Say the numbers out loud.

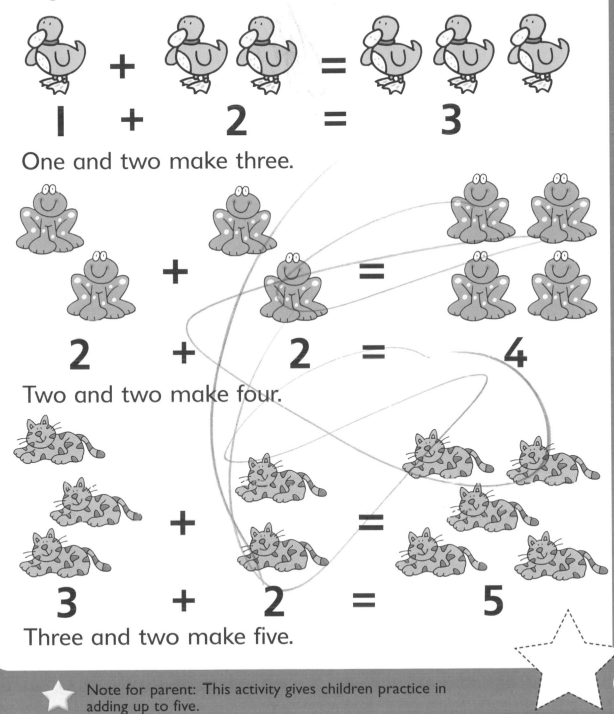

1 + 2 = 3

One and two make three.

2 + 2 = 4

Two and two make four.

3 + 2 = 5

Three and two make five.

Note for parent: This activity gives children practice in adding up to five.

Three more

Colour three more boats.

How many boats are there altogether?

Colour three more trees.

How many trees are there altogether?

Note for parent: This activity gives further practice with adding.

Add three

Point to each picture and count the objects.
Say the numbers out loud.

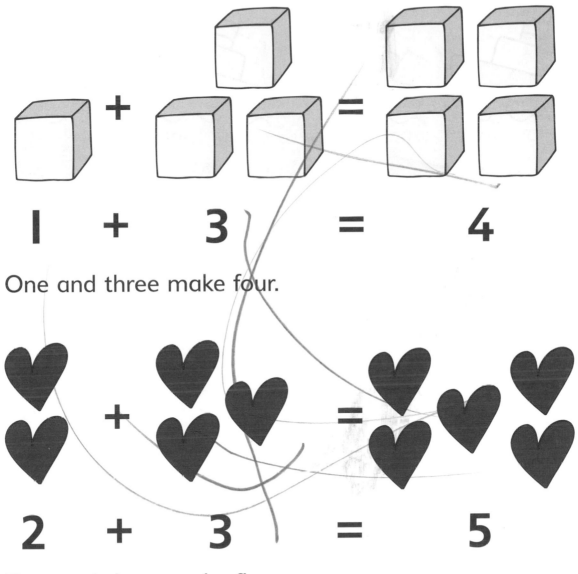

1 + 3 = 4

One and three make four.

2 + 3 = 5

Two and three make five.

Note for parent: Building brick towers is an excellent way to make number work fun.

Four more

Colour four more stars.

How many stars are there altogether?

Colour four more cars.

How many cars are there altogether?

Note for parent: This activity gives further practice with adding things or objects.

Add four

Point to each picture and count the objects.
Say the numbers out loud.

1 + 4 = 5

One and four make five.

1 + 4 = 5

One and four make five.

Note for parent:
Encourage your child to use his or her fingers to count,
add and subtract.

Most

Look at the pictures. Draw a line to join the two children with the same number of cakes.

Draw a ring around the child with the most cakes.

More or less?

Count the ladybirds' spots.
Tick the ladybird with one less spot.

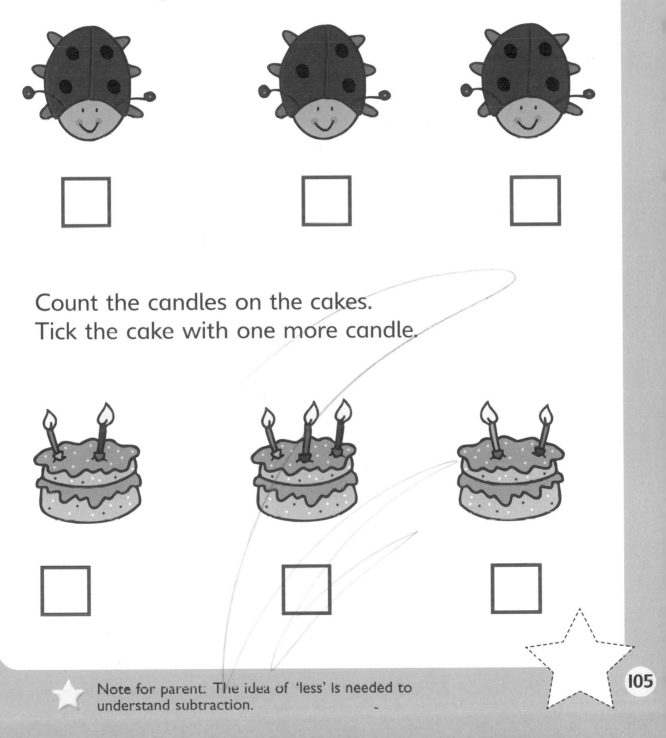

Count the candles on the cakes.
Tick the cake with one more candle.

Note for parent: The idea of 'less' is needed to understand subtraction.

Take one away

Point to each picture and count the objects.
Write the missing numbers in the boxes.

5

take one away leaves

[   ] take one away leaves

Note for parent: Use real objects to practise taking away.

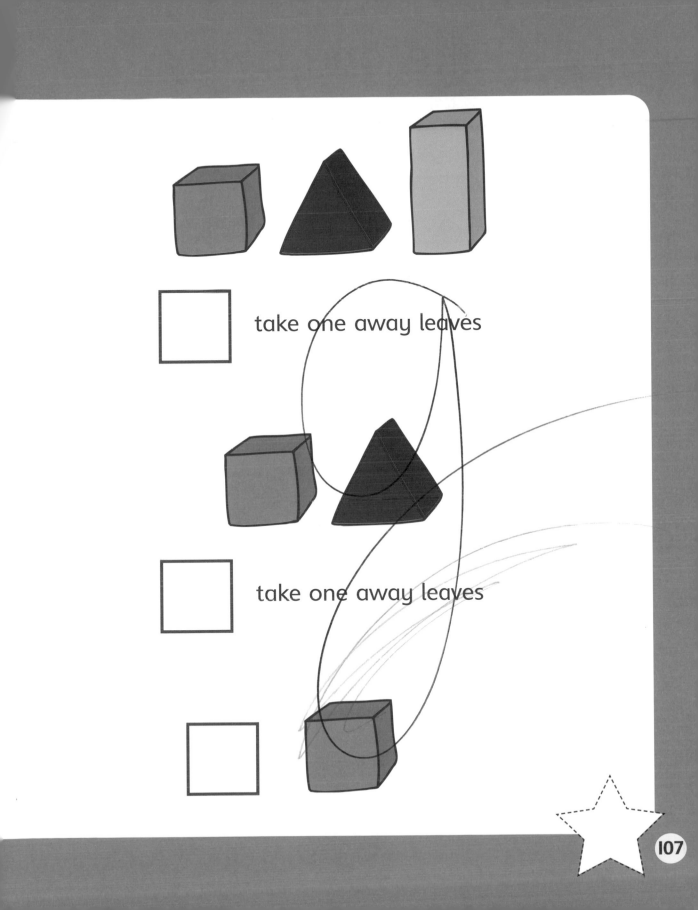

take one away leaves

take one away leaves

Take two away

Look at the picture. Cross two crayons out. How many are left? Draw the answer in the box.

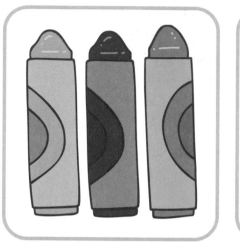

Burst two balloons by crossing them out. How many are left? Draw the answer in the box.

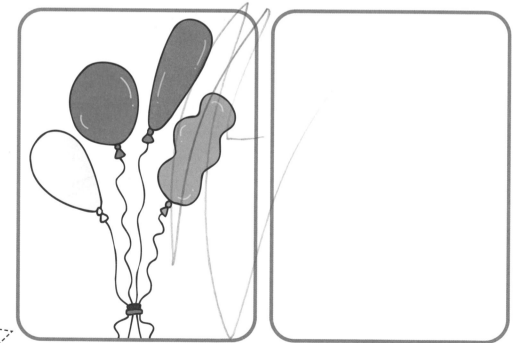

Note for parent: Activities such as these introduce your child to subtraction in a practical way.

How many are left?

Look at the picture. Pick three apples.
How many are left on the tree?
Colour them in. Write your answer in the box.

Take four cakes. How many are left?
Colour it in. Write your answer in the box.

109

Five little ducks

Point to each picture and count the objects.
Write the missing numbers in the boxes.

5

Five little ducks went swimming one day,
Over the pond and far away.
Mother Duck said quack, quack, quack, quack,
But only four little ducks came back.

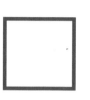

Four little ducks...

Note for parent: This activity gives further practice in counting to 5.

Three little ducks...

Two little ducks...

One little duck...

Take away three

Cross out three fruits from each set. Write how many are left in each set.

Note for parent: These activities help develop your child's understanding of subtraction.

Pick the flowers

Cross out three flowers from each bunch. Write how many flowers are left in each bunch.

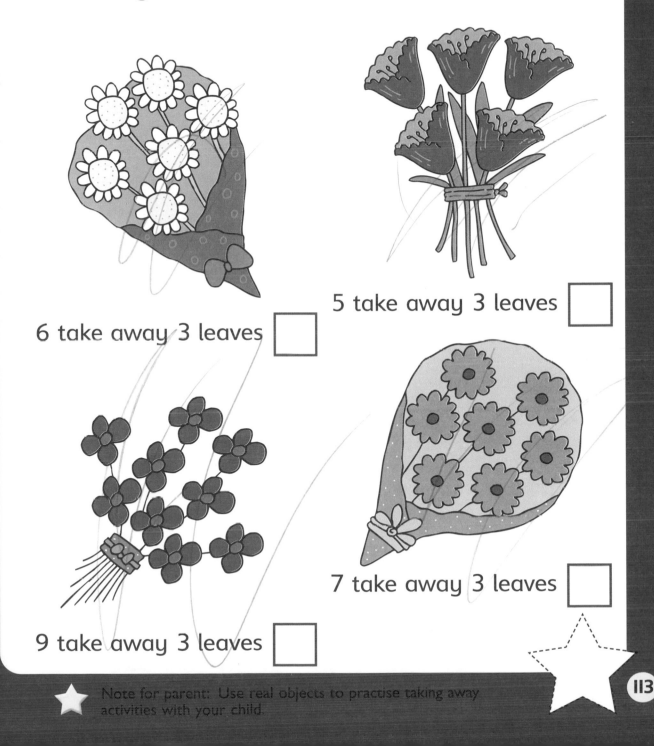

6 take away 3 leaves ☐

5 take away 3 leaves ☐

9 take away 3 leaves ☐

7 take away 3 leaves ☐

Note for parent: Use real objects to practise taking away activities with your child.

Counting down

Count down the ladder and down the rocket. Write in the missing numbers.

start

10
9

7

5

2
1

end

start

10

8

6

4

1

blast off!

Note for parent: Counting down is a skill that helps with subtraction.

On the move

Write in the missing numbers

10   9   ☐   7   ☐   ☐

6   5   ☐   3   ☐   ☐

8   ☐   ☐   5   ☐   3

7   ☐   5   ☐   3   ☐

Note for parent: Practise counting down from different numbers.

Take away four

Cross out four animals from each set.
Write how many are left.

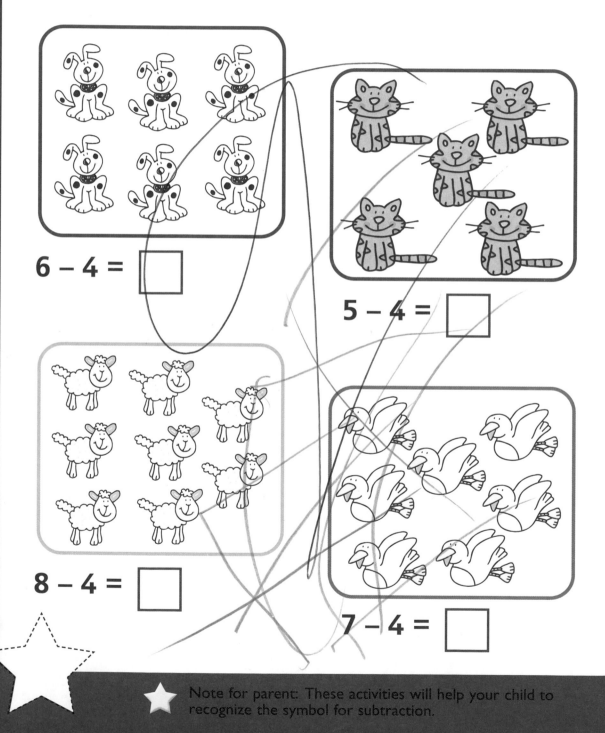

6 – 4 = ☐

5 – 4 = ☐

8 – 4 = ☐

7 – 4 = ☐

Note for parent: These activities will help your child to recognize the symbol for subtraction.

Pop the balloons

Pop four balloons from each bunch by crossing them out. Write how many are left.

$9 - 4 = \boxed{}$

$10 - 4 = \boxed{}$

$4 - 4 = \boxed{}$

Note for parent: Your child should begin to use the zero symbol, 0, for 'none' or 'nothing'.

Take away five

Cross out five things in each box.
Write how many are left.

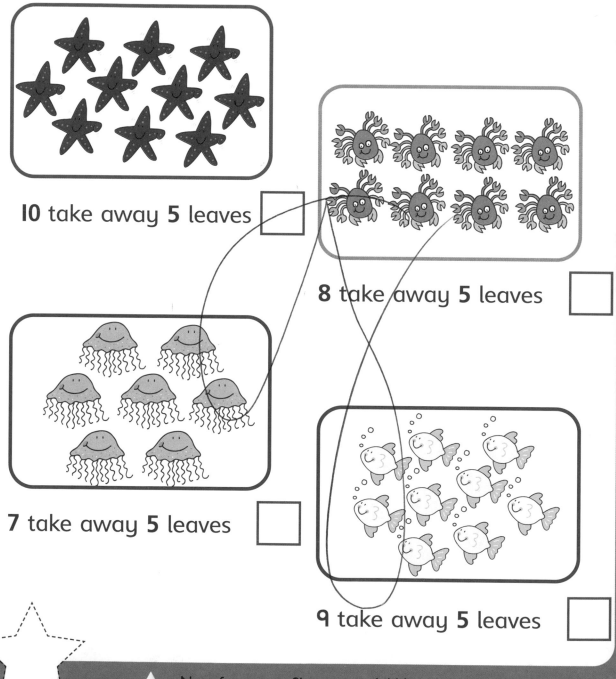

10 take away 5 leaves ☐

8 take away 5 leaves ☐

7 take away 5 leaves ☐

9 take away 5 leaves ☐

Note for parent: Show your child how to use their fingers
to subtract by counting down from the starting number.

Ten green bottles

Cross out five bottles on each wall. Write how many are left.

10 – 5 = ☐

6 – 5 = ☐

9 – 5 = ☐

5 – 5 = ☐

119

In between

What numbers come in between? In each line draw the correct number of shapes and write the number.

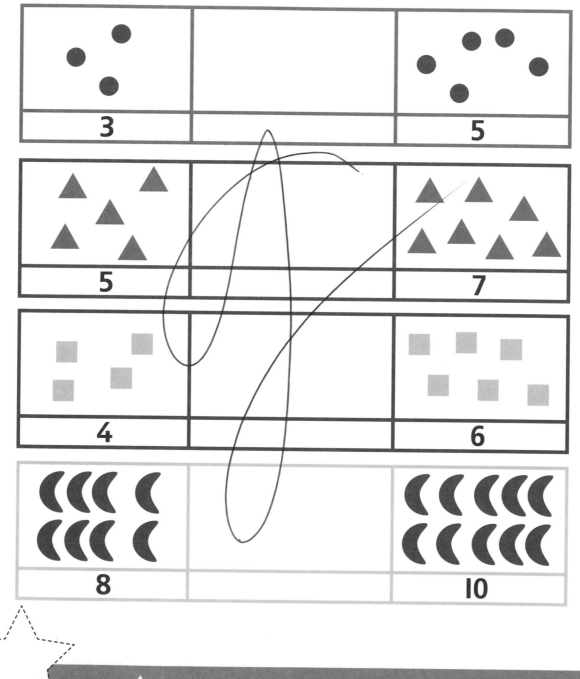

Note for parent: Play a verbal question and answer game: "What number comes in between … and …?"

Practice page

Practise writing the numbers 1 to 10.

Note for parent: Remember, start writing each number at the top.

Letter sounds **a–m**

Trace each letter. Draw a ring around two pictures in each row that begin with the same sound.

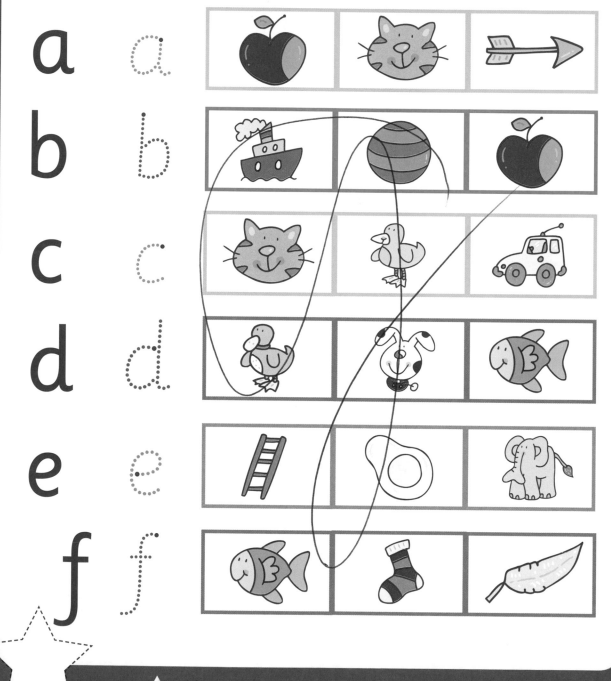

Note for parent: This activity helps children to understand beginning sounds and to write them.

g

h

i

j

k

l

m

Letter sounds **n–z**

Trace each letter. Draw a ring around two pictures in each row that begin with the same sound.

Note for parent: This activity helps children to understand beginning sounds and to write them.

t t

u u

v v

w w

x x

y y

z z

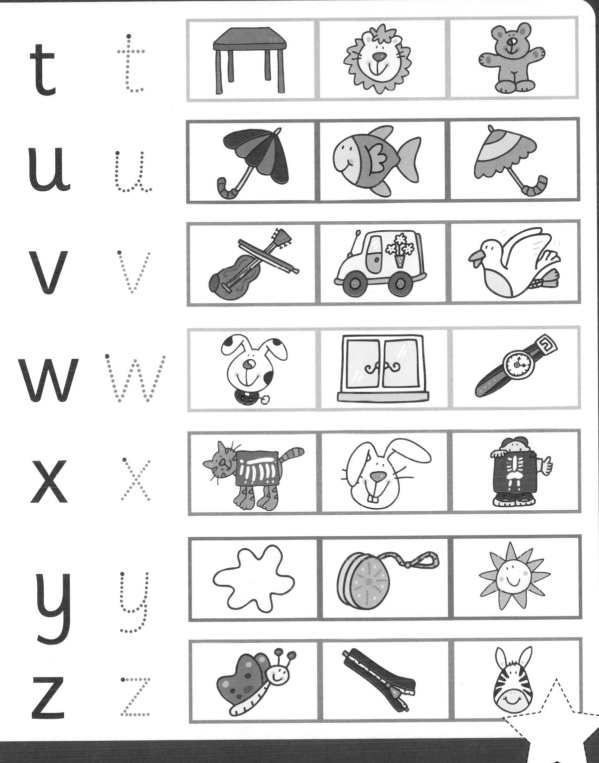

125

Alphabetical order

Join the letters of the alphabet to make these pictures.

Note for parent: This activity helps to teach alphabetical order.

o p q r s t

u v w x y z

Find the pictures

Say the sound of each letter. Look at the big picture and name something beginning with each sound.

d b h k
c a s f

Note for parent: This activity helps children to learn the beginning sounds a, b, c, d, f, h, k and s.

Which letter?

Look at each picture. Choose the right letter and write it in the space to complete each word.

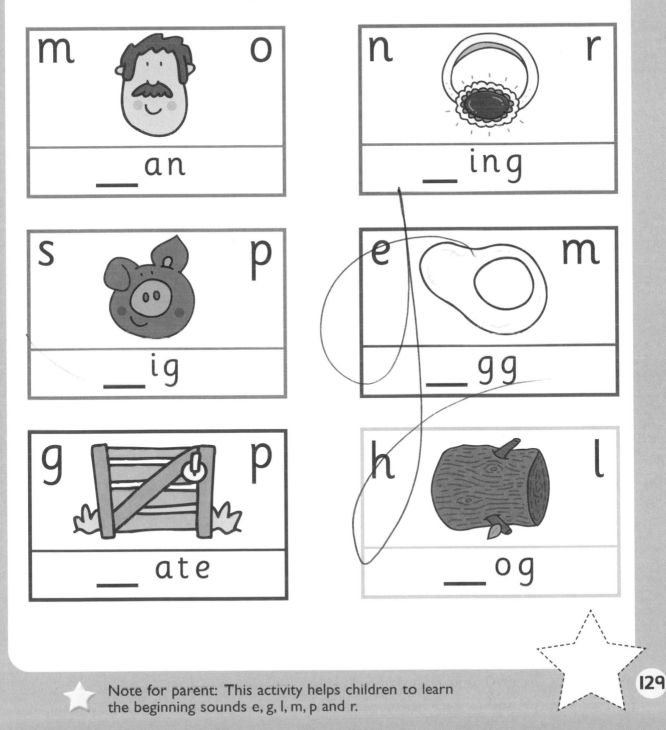

m   o

_ an

n   r

_ ing

s   p

_ ig

e   m

_ gg

g   p

_ ate

h   l

_ og

129

Capital letters

Trace each capital letter and write the matching small one beside it. The first one has been done for you.

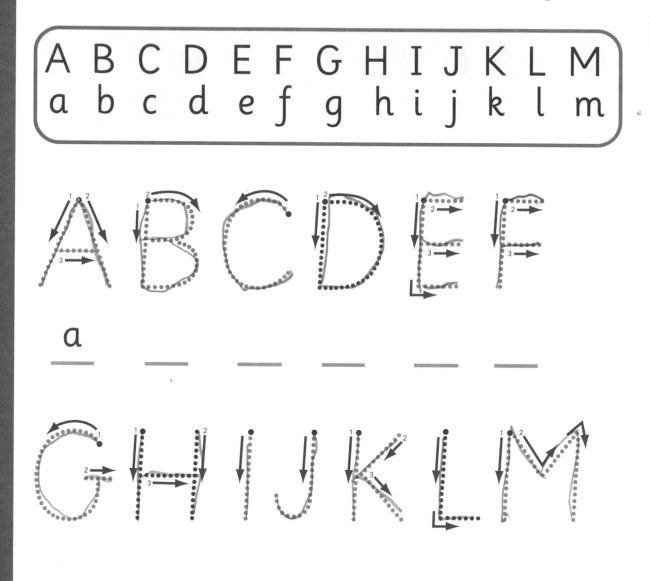

A B C D E F G H I J K L M
a b c d e f g h i j k l m

a

Note for parent: This activity helps children to recognize and write capital letters.

N O P Q R S T U V W X Y Z
n o p q r s t u v w x y z

Beginning sounds

Say the sound of each letter. Look at the big picture and name something beginning with each sound.

n z t f

w o v k

Second chance

Draw lines to join two pictures to each letter.

a   b   c   d

Write the capital letters.

a	f	h	w	p	b	e

Note for parent: This page gives a chance to see what children can remember from earlier pages.

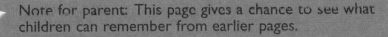

Begins the same

Say the name of the picture in the middle of each box. Draw lines to join each middle picture to other pictures in the box that begin the same way.

Note for parent: This activity encourages children to speak clearly.

Choose a letter

Choose the right letter from the boxes below to complete each word.

f	h	t	b	k	z

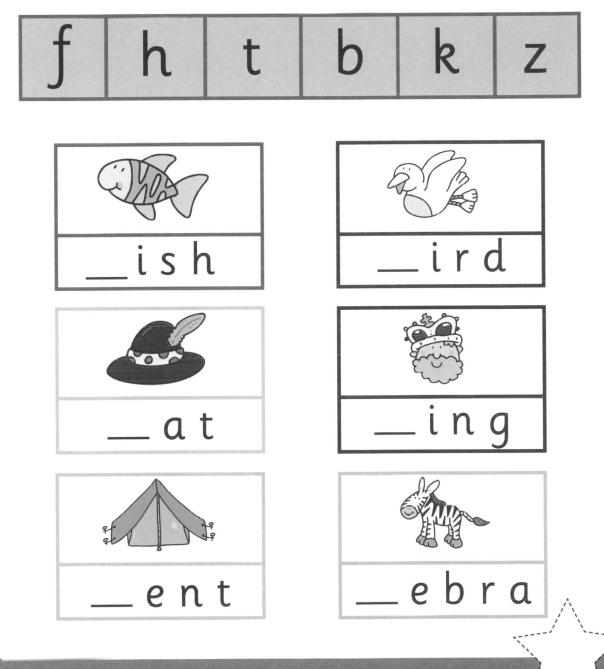

___ i s h

___ i r d

___ a t

___ i n g

___ e n t

___ e b r a

Note for parent: This activity helps children to recognize the beginning sounds b, f, h, k, t and z.

Find a rhyme

Draw lines to join the pictures that rhyme.

Note for parent: Recognizing rhyme helps children
to listen carefully.

In the same way

Say the name of the picture in the middle of each box. Draw lines to join each middle picture to other pictures that begin in the same way.

Note for parent: This activity encourages children to speak clearly.

Learning **b** and **d**

Trace over the letters.

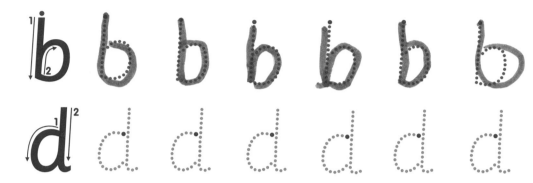

Choose the letter **b** or **d** to complete the words below.

_ice   _aby   _og   _oor

_all   _ook   _uck   _ed

Note for parent: Children often confuse the letters b and d. This activity will help them to learn the difference.

Sound the same

Draw lines to join the pictures that begin in the same way.

Odd one out

Cross out the odd picture inside each shape.

Note for parent: This activity helps children to recognize differences between beginning sounds.

More than one

Write the missing words. Remember to add the letter **s** at the end because there is more than one object.

hat

____

sock

_____

bat

____

ball

_____

tree

_____

star

_____

Note for parent: This activity helps children to learn how to write plurals.

Word endings

Say the name of each picture. Draw a ring around the letter that comes at the end of each word.

Note to parent: This activity encourages children to listen carefully to sounds at the end of words.

Do they rhyme?

Do these pictures rhyme? Put a ✔ or a ✖ in the box under each pair of pictures.

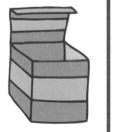

 Note for parent: Recognizing rhymes develops good listening skills.

143

Finding words

Read the words under the pictures. Find the correct letters in the row of mixed-up letters and draw a ring around each one. Write the words in the spaces.

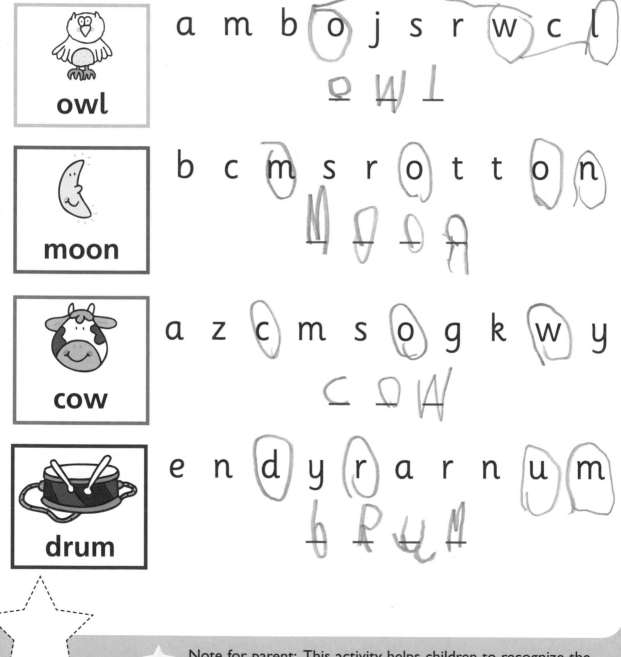

owl

a m b (o) j s r (w) c (l)

owl

moon

b c (m) s r (o) t t (o) (n)

moon

cow

a z (c) m s (o) g k (w) y

cow

drum

e n (d) y r a r n (u) m

drum

Note for parent: This activity helps children to recognize the letters that make up an individual word.

Second chance

Draw lines to join the pictures that rhyme.

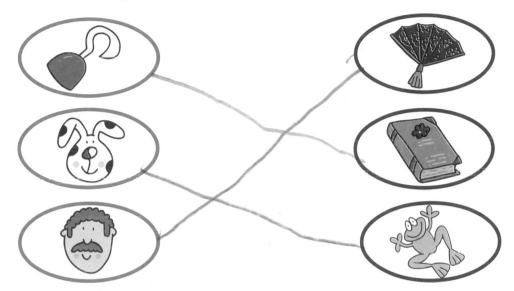

Cross out the picture in this row that does not belong.

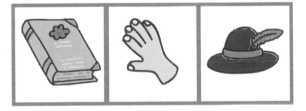

Draw a ring around the letter that comes at the end of each word.

Note for parent: This page tests what children remember from earlier pages.

Sounds in the middle

Trace over the letters. Say the sounds.

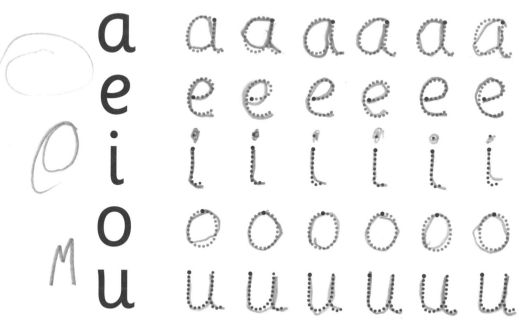

Name each picture. Tick the words with an **a** sound in the middle.

Name each picture. Tick the words with an **e** sound in the middle.

Note to parent: This activity helps children to identify the vowels a, e, i, o and u.

Name each picture. Tick the words with
an **i** sound in the middle.

Name each picture. Tick the words with
an **o** sound in the middle.

Name each picture. Tick the words with
a **u** sound in the middle.

At the beginning

Name each picture. Draw a ring around the correct beginning sound.

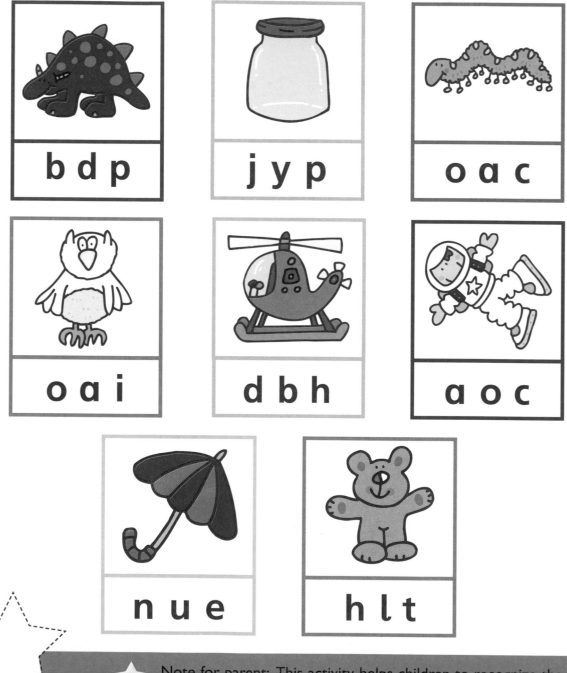

b d p

j y p

o a c

o a i

d b h

a o c

n u e

h l t

Note for parent: This activity helps children to recognize the letters a, c, d, h, j, o, t and u.

Little words

Find the little words in the grid below.
Draw a ring around each word you find.

so	is	it	on	at
me	go	no	if	we

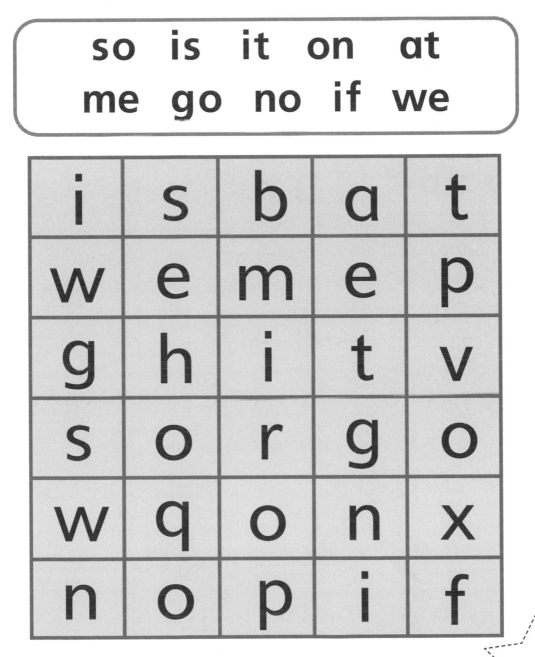

i	s	b	a	t
w	e	m	e	p
g	h	i	t	v
s	o	r	g	o
w	q	o	n	x
n	o	p	i	f

Final sounds

Use the letters from the box to finish the words.

d   t   g   x   n   p

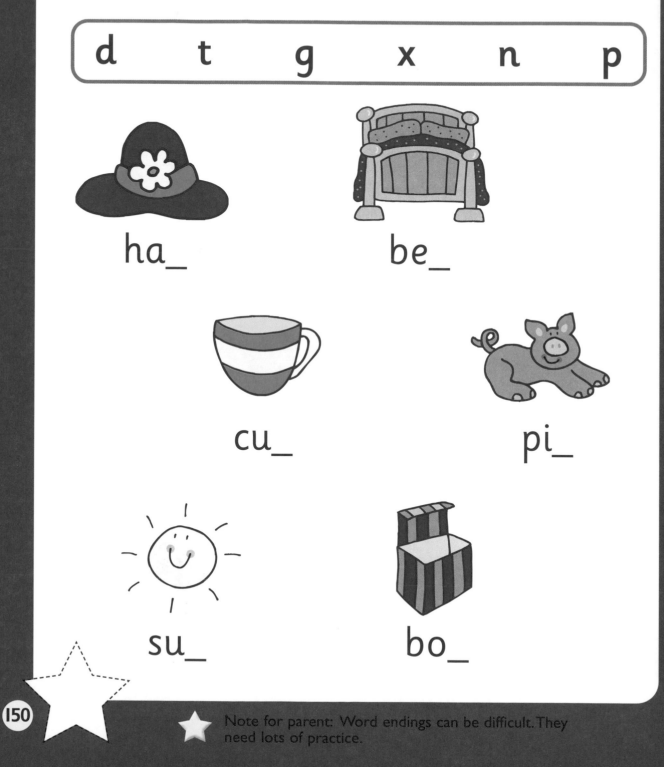

ha_

be_

cu_

pi_

su_

bo_

Note for parent: Word endings can be difficult. They need lots of practice.

Fishing game

Trace the dots to write the letters. Say the sounds.
Join each fish to the boat with the same sound.

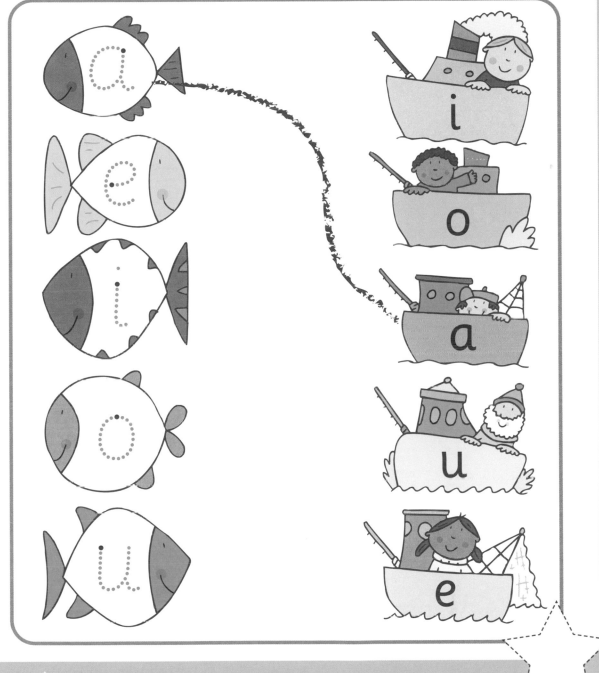

Note for parent: This activity helps your child identify
the vowels a, e, i, o and u.

Jigsaw words

Match the jigsaw pieces to make the words.

Note for parent: Sound out familiar three-letter words with your child.

Does it fit?

Say the sound of each letter. Ring the odd one out in each row.

d	d	d	b	d	d
p	p	q	p	p	p
b	d	b	b	b	b
q	q	q	p	q	q
h	h	h	h	h	n
a	a	o	a	a	a
o	o	o	o	a	o

Note for parent: Recognizing d, b, p and q needs lots of practice, as they all look similar.

Join the dots

Join the dots in the right order. Begin with **a**.

a b c d e f g h i j k

What can you see?

Note for parent: Practise saying the alphabet with your child.

What is it?

Join the dots in the right order. Begin with l.

l m n o p q r s t u v w x y z

What can you see?

Note for parent: Make some similar dot-to-dot puzzles for your child to complete.

Spot the sound

Tick the things that start with a **ch** sound.
Draw a ring around the things that start with
a **sh** sound.

Note for parent: This activity compares the
double sounds sh and ch.

Practise **sh** and **ch**

Write **ch** or **sh** to start or finish each word.

fi _ _

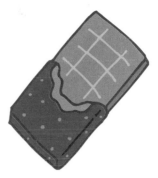

_ _ocolate

_ _ e e p

chur_ _

s p l a _ _

_ _ick

Note for parent: Emphasize the ch and sh sounds as you say each word.

Right or wrong?

Put a tick or a cross in each box.   ✔ **yes**   ✘ **no**

begins with **sh**   ☐

begins with **sh**   ☐

begins with **ch**   ☐

begins with **sh**   ☐

begins with **ch**   ☐

begins with **ch**   ☐

Note for parent: Say each word with your child. Help them to distinguish the sh and ch sounds.

Picture quiz

Say the name of each picture. Listen to the starting sounds. Circle the odd one out in each row.

Note for parent: This activity introduces the double sound th as well as ch and sh.

Writing numbers

Count the dots. Write the numbers.

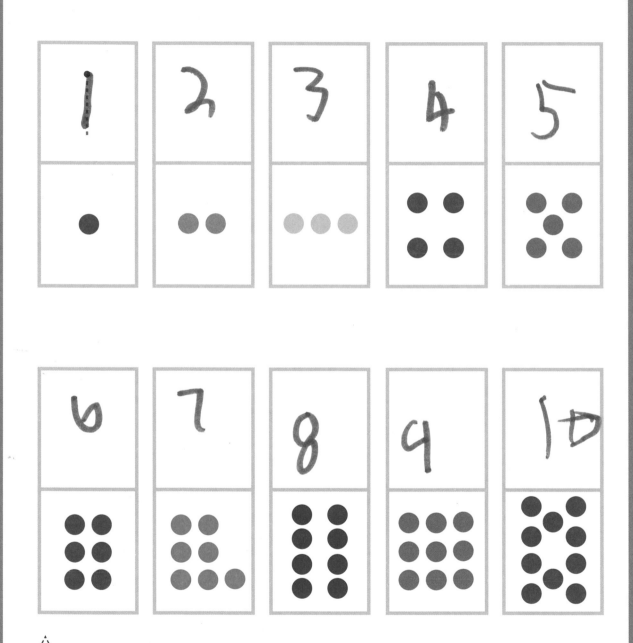

Note for parent: Playing dominoes and similar number games will develop your child's number skills.

Number words

Read the number words. Join each word to the right number.

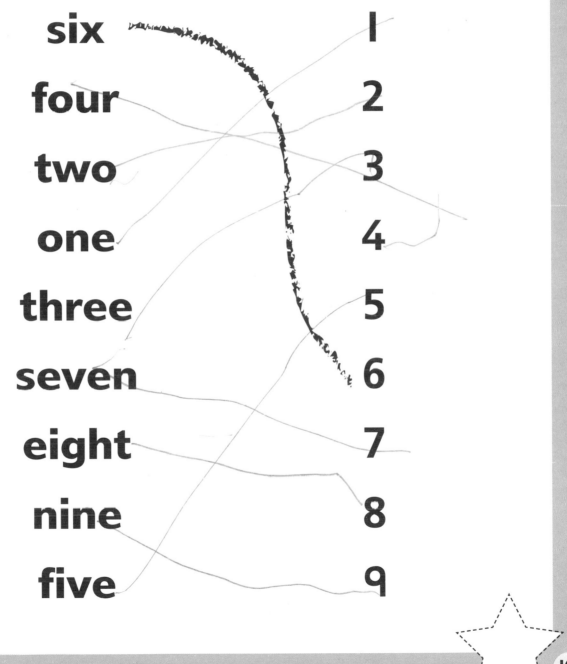

six	1
four	2
two	3
one	4
three	5
seven	6
eight	7
nine	8
five	9

161

Counting

Count the objects. Join each set to the right number.

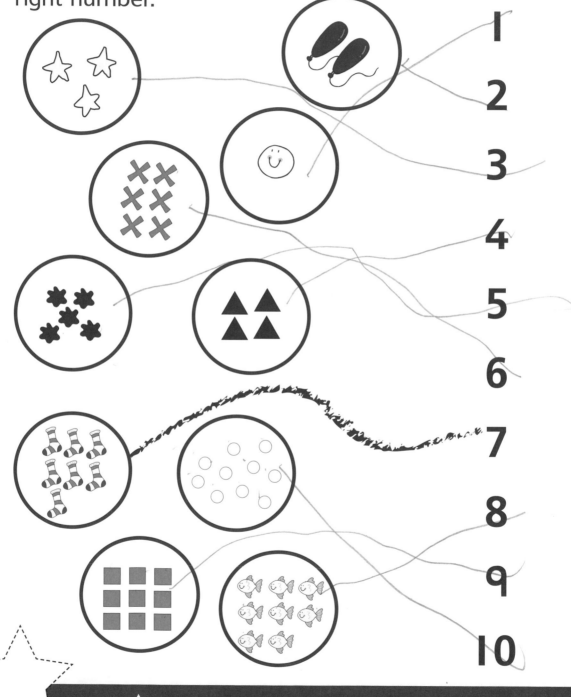

1
2
3
4
5
6
7
8
9
10

Note for parent: Children often find it more difficult to count objects that are not in tidy rows.

One to ten

Read and say the number words.

one	
two	
three	
four	
five	
six	
seven	
eight	
nine	
ten	

Learn this rhyme:

> One, two, three, four, five,
> Once I caught a fish alive,
> Six, seven, eight, nine, ten,
> Then I let it go again.

Note for parent: Number songs and rhymes reinforce number names and sequences.

Adding

Fill in the missing numbers to complete these sums.

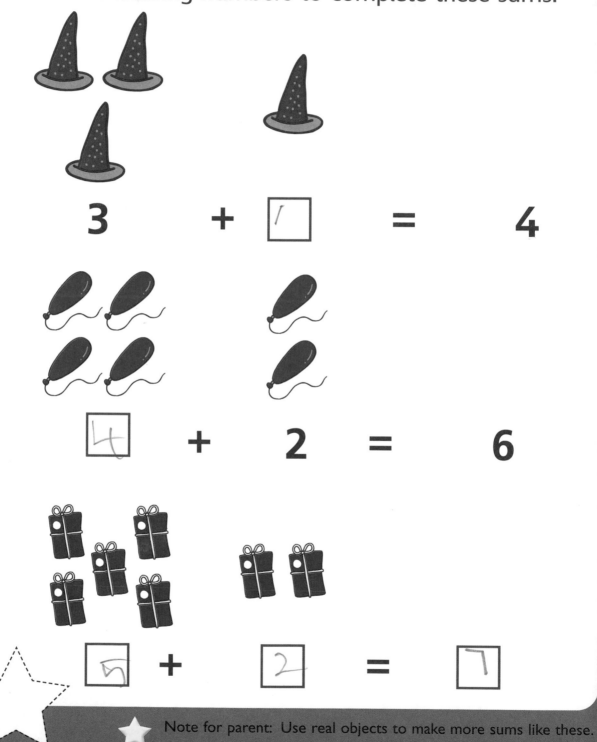

3 + [1] = 4

[4] + 2 = 6

[5] + [2] = [7]

Note for parent: Use real objects to make more sums like these.

Threading beads

Write the numbers 1 to 10 on these beads.

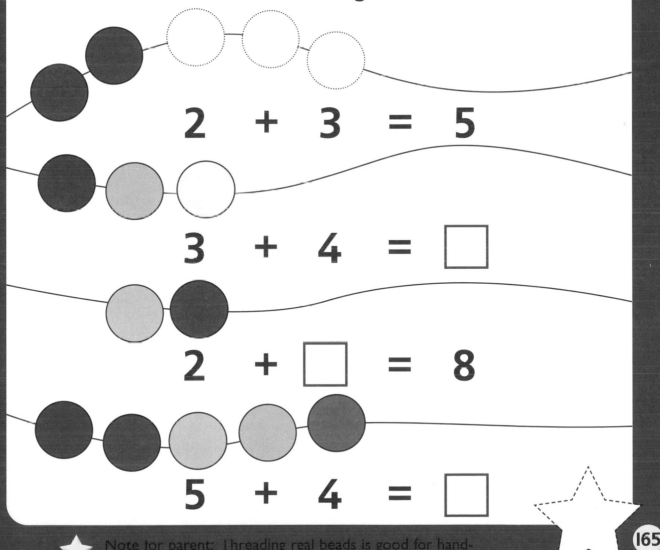

Draw the right number of beads to complete each sum. Write in the missing numbers.

$2 + 3 = 5$

$3 + 4 = \boxed{}$

$2 + \boxed{} = 8$

$5 + 4 = \boxed{}$

Note for parent: Threading real beads is good for hand-eye co-ordination, as well as for practising number skills.

Subtracting

Read these number stories.
Write in the missing numbers.

Sarah had **5** lollies.
She ate **1**.
She had ☐ **4** left.

Shane had **10** conkers.
He gave **3** away.
He had ☐ **7** left.

Anne had **7** crayons.
She lost **2**.
She had ☐ **5** left.

Ben had **8** cherries.
He ate **4**.
He had ☐ **4** left.

Note for parent: Encourage your child to tell their own number stories.

Count the dots

Write the missing numbers.

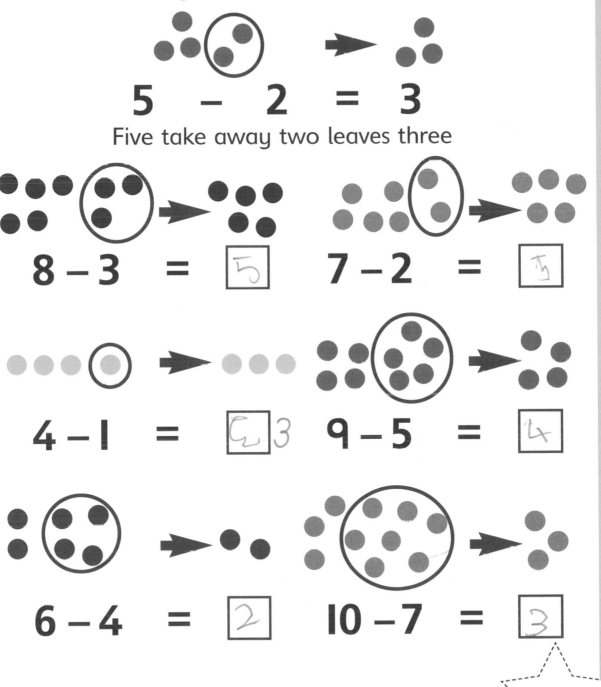

$$5 - 2 = 3$$

Five take away two leaves three

$$8 - 3 = \boxed{5}$$

$$7 - 2 = \boxed{5}$$

$$4 - 1 = \boxed{3}$$

$$9 - 5 = \boxed{4}$$

$$6 - 4 = \boxed{2}$$

$$10 - 7 = \boxed{3}$$

Note for parent: Practise this activity with real objects such as toys.

Counting on

Count on along the number tracks to do these sums. Write in the answers.

$$1 + 2 = \boxed{}$$

| 1 | 2 | 3 | 4 | 5 | 6 | 7 | 8 | 9 | 10 |

$$3 + 4 = \boxed{}$$

| 1 | 2 | 3 | 4 | 5 | 6 | 7 | 8 | 9 | 10 |

$$5 + 3 = \boxed{}$$

| 1 | 2 | 3 | 4 | 5 | 6 | 7 | 8 | 9 | 10 |

$$7 + 2 = \boxed{}$$

| 1 | 2 | 3 | 4 | 5 | 6 | 7 | 8 | 9 | 10 |

Note for parent: Show your child how to move their finger along the number track as they count on or back to do each sum.

Counting back

Count back along the number tracks to do these subtractions. Write in the answers.

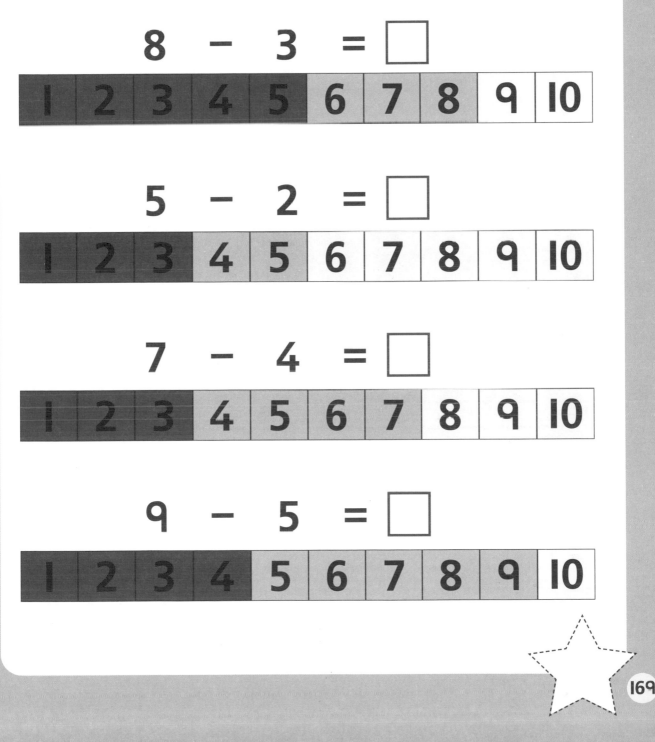

8 − 3 = ☐

| 1 | 2 | 3 | 4 | 5 | 6 | 7 | 8 | 9 | 10 |

5 − 2 = ☐

| 1 | 2 | 3 | 4 | 5 | 6 | 7 | 8 | 9 | 10 |

7 − 4 = ☐

| 1 | 2 | 3 | 4 | 5 | 6 | 7 | 8 | 9 | 10 |

9 − 5 = ☐

| 1 | 2 | 3 | 4 | 5 | 6 | 7 | 8 | 9 | 10 |

Hidden numbers

There are nine ducks in each line, but some are hidden. Write down how many are hidden.

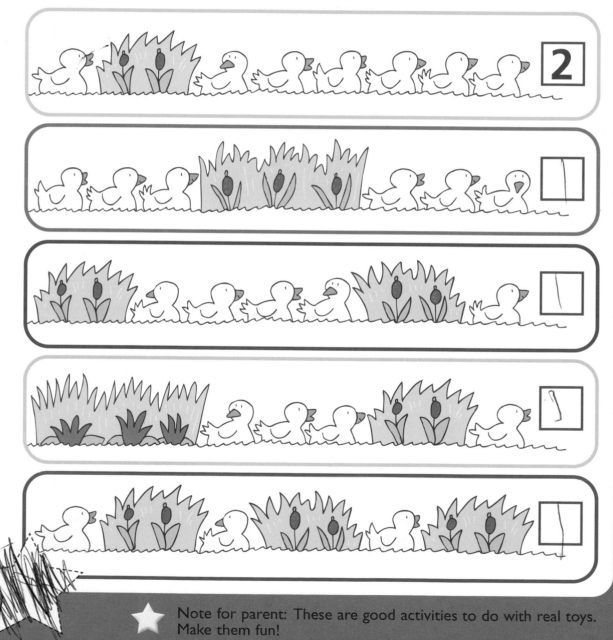

Note for parent: These are good activities to do with real toys. Make them fun!

What's the total?

Count the different crayons. How many are there in each jar? Write down the totals.

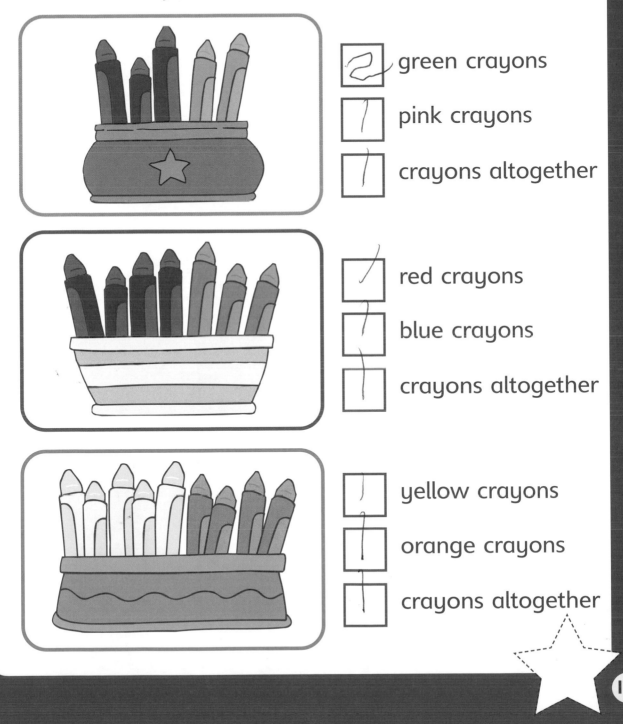

green crayons

pink crayons

crayons altogether

red crayons

blue crayons

crayons altogether

yellow crayons

orange crayons

crayons altogether

Ten buttons

Each coat should have ten buttons. Draw the missing buttons and write the missing numbers.

| 7 | and | | make | 10 |

| | and | | make | 10 |

| | and | | make | 10 |

| | and | | make | 10 |

Note for parent: Prompt your child to look at the two rows of buttons. Draw the missing buttons in the gaps.

Doubles

Double the number of circles in each row. Write down the new totals.

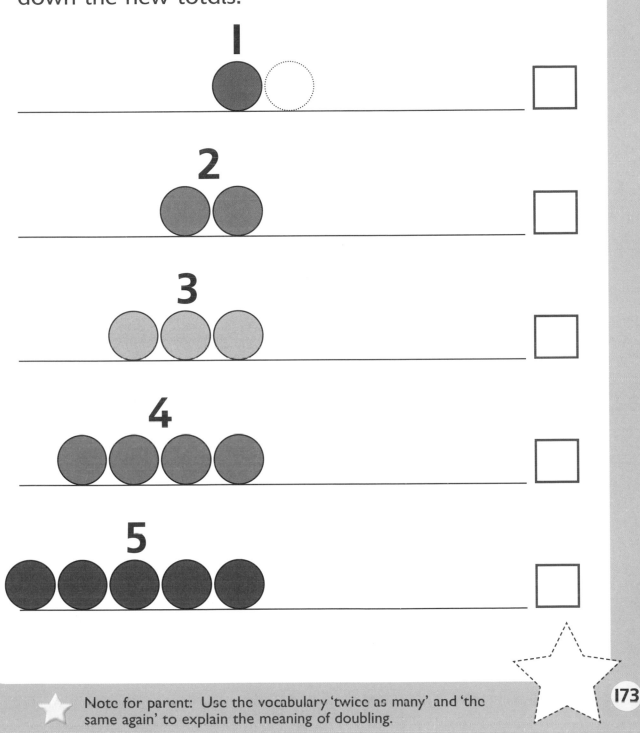

1

2

3

4

5

Note for parent: Use the vocabulary 'twice as many' and 'the same again' to explain the meaning of doubling.

Flat shapes

Join each shape to its name.

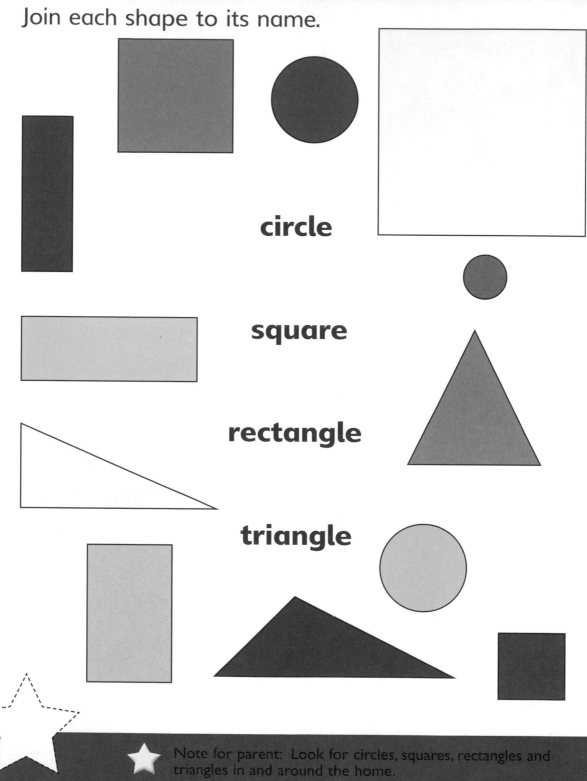

circle

square

rectangle

triangle

Note for parent: Look for circles, squares, rectangles and triangles in and around the home.

Shapes and sizes

Tick the largest shape in each box.

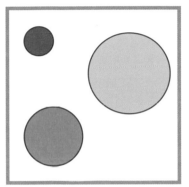 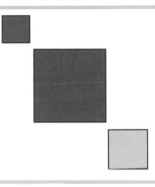 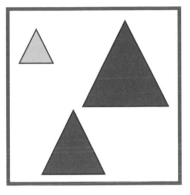

Tick the smallest shape in each box.

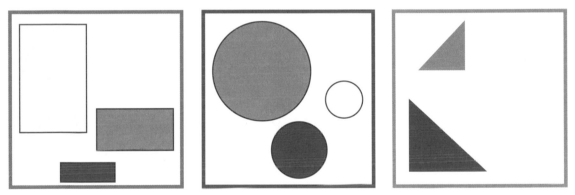

Number these shapes in order of size, biggest first.

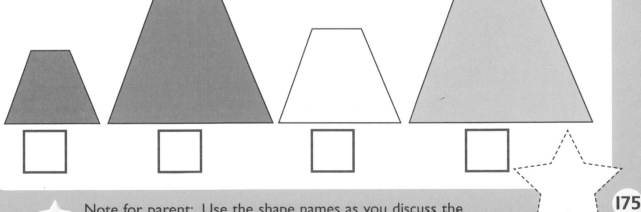

Note for parent: Use the shape names as you discuss the different-sized shapes.

175

Solid shapes

Join each shape to its name.

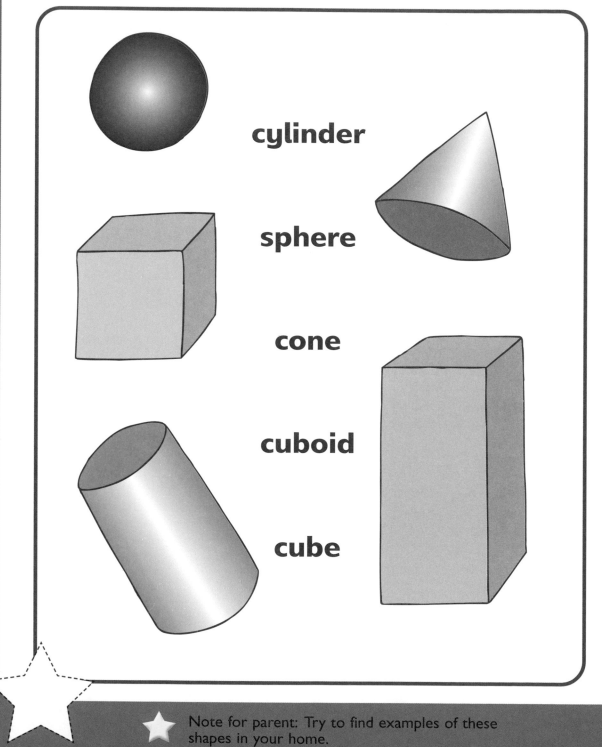

cylinder

sphere

cone

cuboid

cube

Note for parent: Try to find examples of these shapes in your home.

Matching shapes

Draw lines to join the matching shapes.

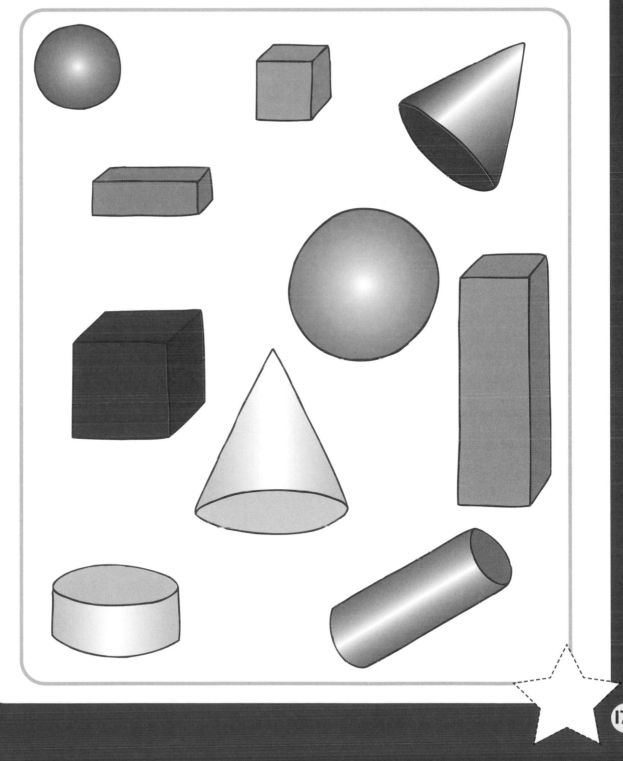

Does it fit?

Draw lines to put each shape in the right place in the puzzle.

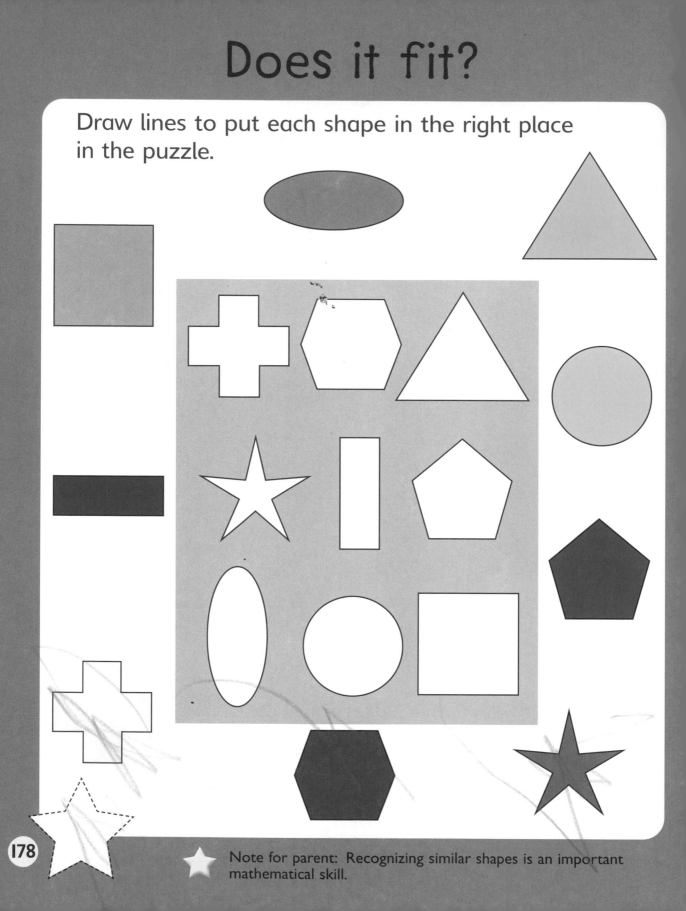

Note for parent: Recognizing similar shapes is an important mathematical skill.

Choose a box

Choose a box to fit each present. Draw lines to match them up.

Halves

Draw the missing half of each thing.

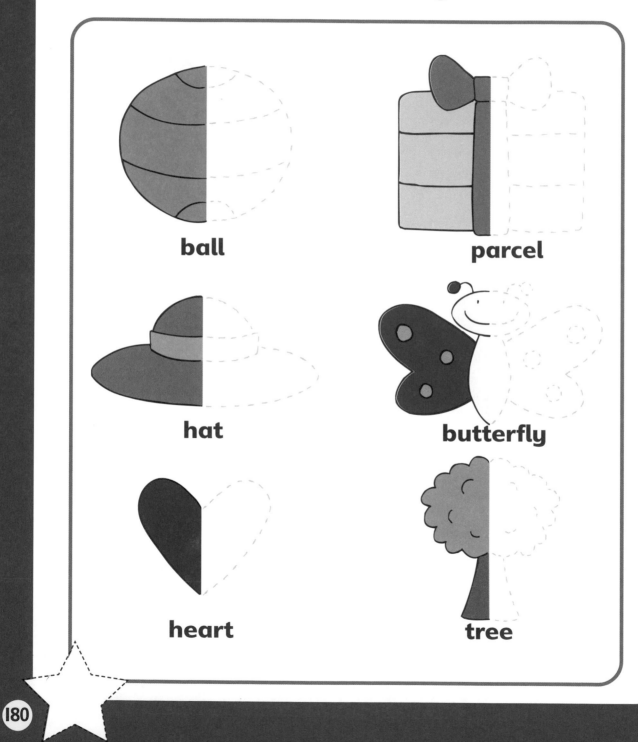

ball

parcel

hat

butterfly

heart

tree

Share it out

Draw lines to cut each thing in half. Make sure you are fair!

Are the sweets shared fairly? Put a tick or a cross.

Money boxes

Count the pennies in each money box. Join the boxes to the right totals.

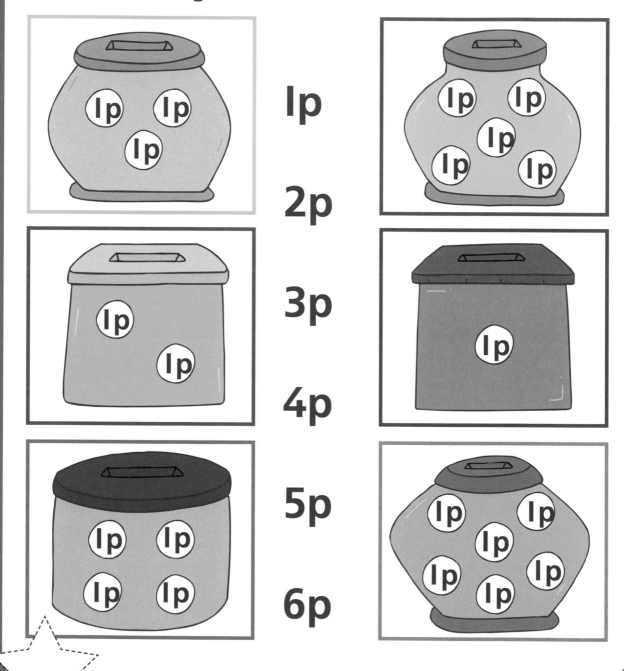

1p

2p

3p

4p

5p

6p

Note for parent: Draw around and count real coins with your child.

At the market

Each fruit costs **1p**. Draw the right number of pennies to pay for each basket of fruit.

Spending money

Count the coins to find the totals.

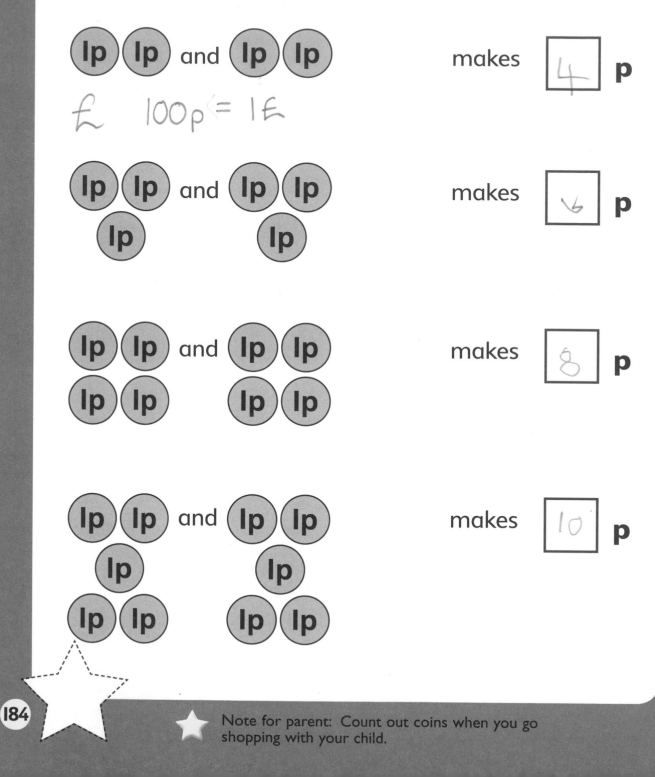

1p 1p and 1p 1p   makes   [4] **p**

£ 100p = 1£

1p 1p and 1p 1p
1p   1p   makes   [6] **p**

1p 1p and 1p 1p
1p 1p   1p 1p   makes   [8] **p**

1p 1p and 1p 1p
1p   1p
1p 1p   1p 1p   makes   [10] **p**

Note for parent: Count out coins when you go shopping with your child.

The toy stall

Draw the number of 1p coins you need to buy these toys.

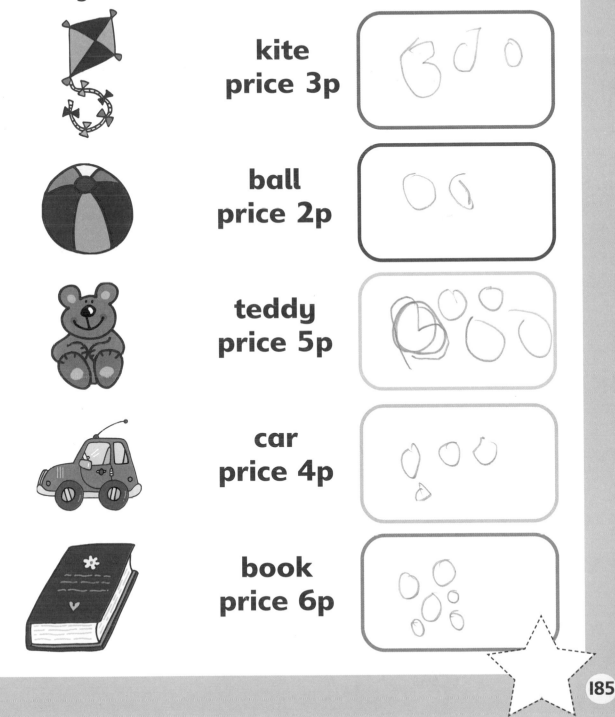

kite
price 3p

ball
price 2p

teddy
price 5p

car
price 4p

book
price 6p

185

Clock face

Trace over the numbers on the clock face.

Note for parent: Point out the difference between the long hand and the short hand.

What's the time?

Join each clock to the right time.

9 o'clock

3 o'clock

12 o'clock

8 o'clock

2 o'clock

6 o'clock

Pretty patterns

Colour the clothes on the lines to make patterns.

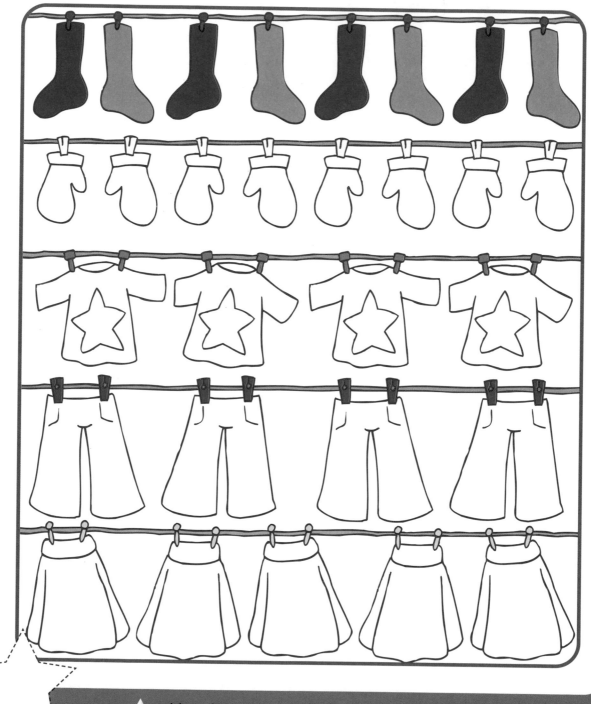

Note for parent: Use beads, toy bricks or other objects to make up colour-, size- or shape-based sequences.

What comes next?

Draw the right shapes to continue the patterns.
Colour the shapes.

Note for parent: Encourage your child to draw shape patterns of their own on blank paper.

Longer or shorter?

Look at this pencil.

Find all the pencils that are longer than this one. Circle them.

What colour is the longest pencil?
What colour is the shortest pencil?

Taller or shorter?

Draw a taller tree.

Draw a shorter tree.

Draw a shorter house.

Draw a taller house.

Draw a circle around the shortest child.

Heavy or light?

Which things are heavy?
Which things are light?
Draw a line from each thing to the right word.

heavy

light

Full, empty or half-full?

Some of these bottles and jars are full. Some are empty. Some are half-full. Draw lines to the right labels.

full   **empty**   **half-full**

Practice page

Find two numbers in each row that add up to **10**. Colour them in. Use the number line at the bottom of the page to help.

10	1	8	2	7	5	4

3	7	8	4	9	5	10

0	6	9	2	7	5	5

10	1	9	5	6	7	8

2	3	0	5	6	4	1

10	9	3	7	8	5	4

0	1	2	3	4	5	6	7	8	9	10

Note for parent: Counting on and back along a number line will help your child with addition and subtraction.

I can do maths

These number robots add and take away.
Write the numbers that come out.

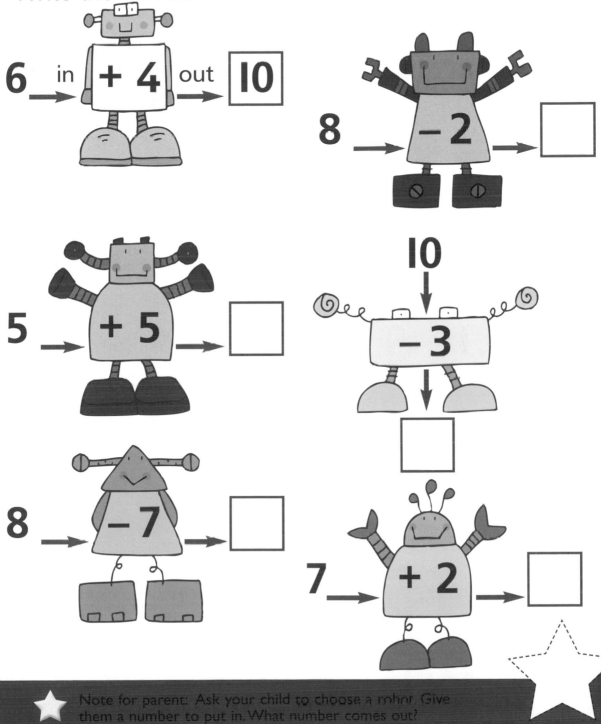

6 in $+4$ out 10

8 -2

5 $+5$

10 -3

8 -7

7 $+2$

Note for parent: Ask your child to choose a robot. Give
them a number to put in. What number comes out?

Real words

Read the words in the tree. Join each word to the right apple.

Note for parent: This activity introduces some key 'high frequency words'.

Read the words in the rocket. Join each word to the right star.

Names

Names begin with a capital letter. Circle the capital letter that starts your name.

A B C D E F G H I
J K L M N O P Q R
S T U V W X Y Z

Now circle the small letters in your name.

a b c d e f g h i
j k l m n o p q r
s t u v w x y z

Write your name here:

_____

Note for parent: Your child should only use a capital for the first letter of their name.

Draw lines to match the children to their mugs.

Write your name on this mug.

Busy bees

Read these words.

on

I

up

at

look

for

he

we

you

like

and

is

said

are

go

Note for parent: This provides more practice in reading high frequency words.

Words and pictures

Draw lines to match the words to the pictures.

mum

cat

dog

tree

house

dad

apple

ball

Is it the same?

Draw a line to match the first word in each row to the same word further along.

look	up	is	you	look	we

and	go	he	and	for	I

play	mum	play	dad	away	at

like	on	said	like	no	day

cat	are	the	going	cat	a

come	this	am	dog	to	come

202

Note for parent: Prompt your child to look at and sound the first letter of each word to help find the word matches.

Big and small

Read the big words. Draw a line to match the big words and the small words.

How does it begin?

Choose the correct letter to begin each word.
Write the letters in place to complete the words.

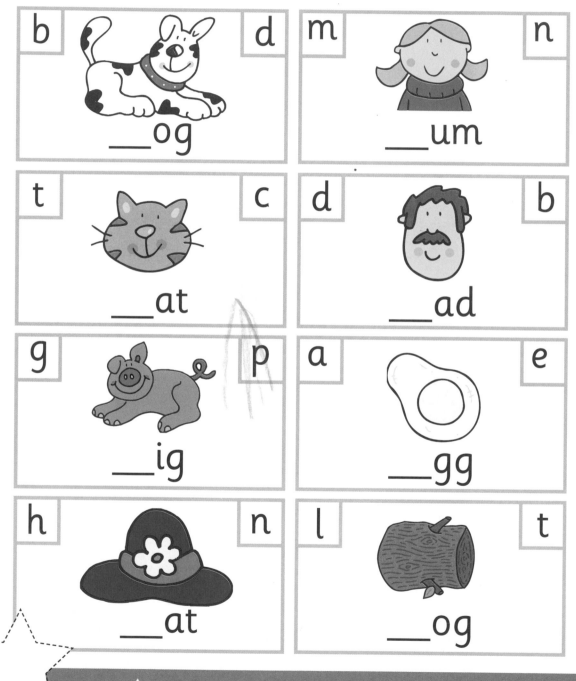

b d ___og

m n ___um

t c ___at

d b ___ad

g p ___ig

a e ___gg

h n ___at

l t ___og

Note for parent: Sound the alternative letters with your child.
Emphasize the starting sound of each word.

Odd one out

Look at the first letter of each word. Put a cross through the odd one out in each row.

dad	**apple**	**dog**
mum	**net**	**mouse**
ball	**door**	**bed**
cat	**car**	**sun**
house	**hat**	**goat**

Word puzzles

Name each picture. Write **a**, **e**, **i**, **o** or **u** in the middle to complete the words in each puzzle.

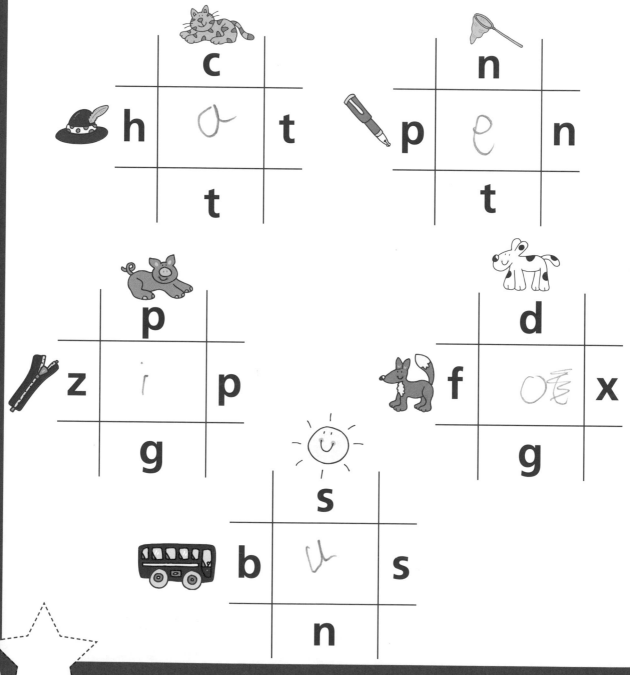

Count the letters in the words. Join each word
to the right truck.

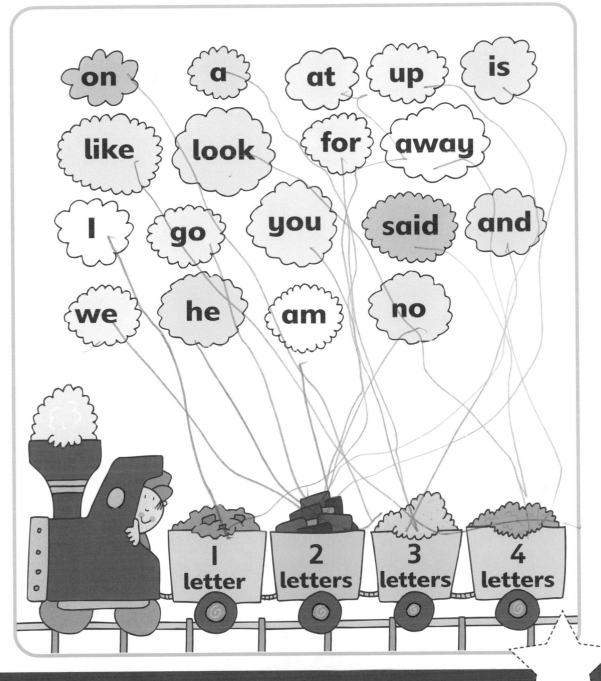

Catch the ball

Read these words. Draw lines to match the balls with the same words.

Note for parent: Praise your child's efforts as they read these high frequency words.

Three-letter words

Read the words. Draw a circle around the word that matches each picture.

cat/cot

pin/pen

fun/fan

dog/dig

man/mum

day/dad

peg/pig

cup/cap

Yes or no?

Listen to each question. Circle the right answer.

Are you a girl?   **yes**   **no**

Are you a boy?   **yes**   **no**

Can you fly?   **yes**   **no**

Do you like ice cream?   **yes**   **no**

Do you like pizza?   **yes**   **no**

Can you read?   **yes**   **no**

Note for parent: Play a yes/no question-and-answer game with your child. Encourage him or her to think of questions to ask you.

House words

Look at the picture. Write in the missing words.

roof

house

window

door

garage

This is a _ _ _ _ _ .

This is a _ _ _ _ .

This is a _ _ _ _ _ _ .

This is a _ _ _ _ .

This is a _ _ _ _ _ _ .

Note for parent: You can also help your child write your house number on the door in the picture.

Word endings

Choose the correct letter to end each word.
Write the letters in place to finish the words.

g · b
do___

f · t
ca___

m · n
mu___

p · d
da___

z · s
bu___

r · w
ca___

Note for parent: Say the words with the alternative endings.
Prompt your child to say which is correct.

Missing words

Use the words in the boxes to complete the sentences. Write them in place.

is	a	cat

This is my _____.

It _____ white.

It has _____ long tail.

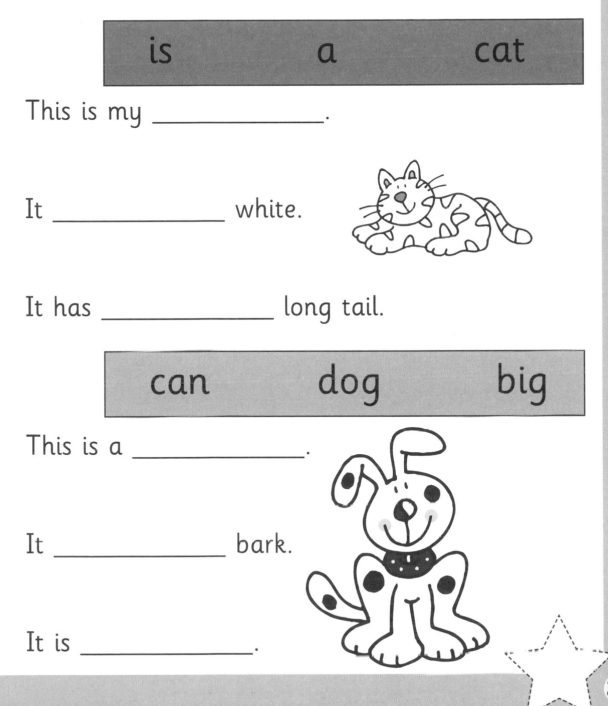

can	dog	big

This is a _____.

It _____ bark.

It is _____.

Read and draw

Circle the word **and** in each box. Draw pictures to match the words.

mum and dad

cat and dog

sun and moon

boy and girl

Note for parent: Point out common words such as 'and' when you read with your child.

Match the words

Write the right words under the pictures.

| bat | pig | rat | dog | cat | hen |

Balloons

Practise reading the words in the balloons.

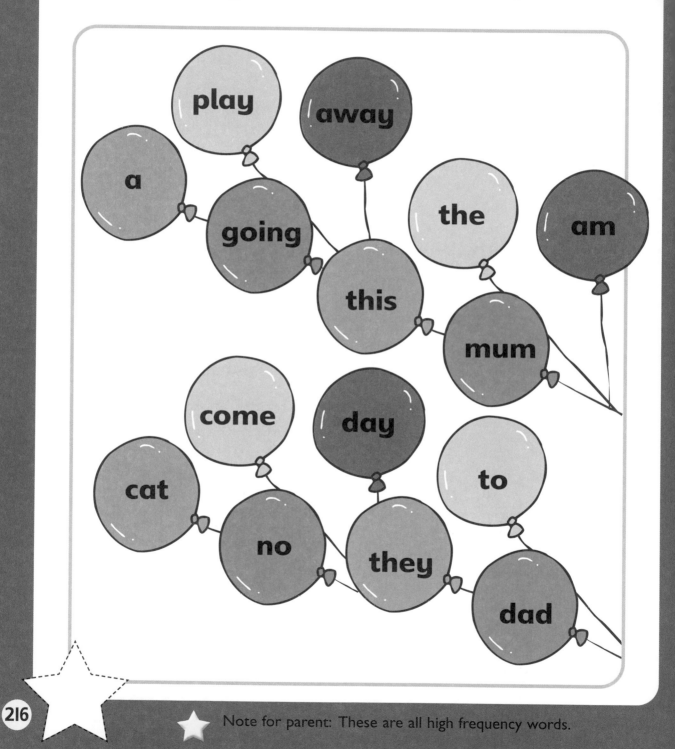

Note for parent: These are all high frequency words.

Sh and ch words

Trace over the letters and say the sounds.

Write **ch** or **sh** to complete these words.

_ _eep

_ _oes

_ _urch

_ _air

Now read the words.

Th words

Trace over the letters and say the sound.

th th th th th

Write **th** to complete these words.

_ _umb

_ _ree

too_ _

ba_ _

_ _ermometer

_ _rone

Double sounds

Read these words. Join the things that start with the same sound.

cheese

thumb

3

three

shark

church

throne

shoes

sheep

cherries

Family words

Help this family to find the right presents.
Draw lines.

mum

dad

baby

granny

cat

mum

granny

dad

baby

cat

Note for parent: Make a list of the members of your family
with your child.

Days of the week

Do you know the days of the week?
What does Lucy do each day?
Trace the letters. Read the name of each day.

Monday

Wednesday

Friday

Tuesday

Thursday

Saturday

Sunday

Note to parent: Tell your child that days of the week always start with a capital letter.

Snakes and ladders

Draw lines to match the same words on each ladder.

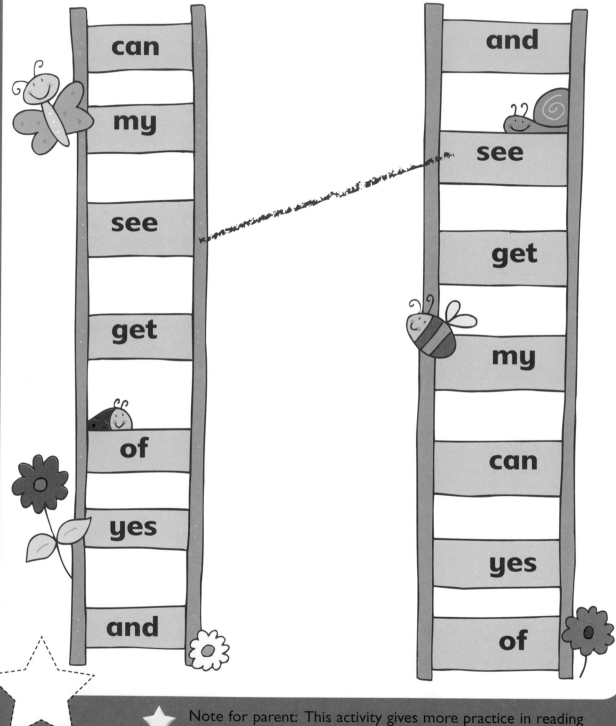

Note for parent: This activity gives more practice in reading high frequency words.

Draw lines to match the same words on each snake.

went

big

me

of

all

she

it

went

me

big

all

of

it

she

True or false?

Is it true or false? Put a tick (✔) for true or a cross (✗) for false in each box.

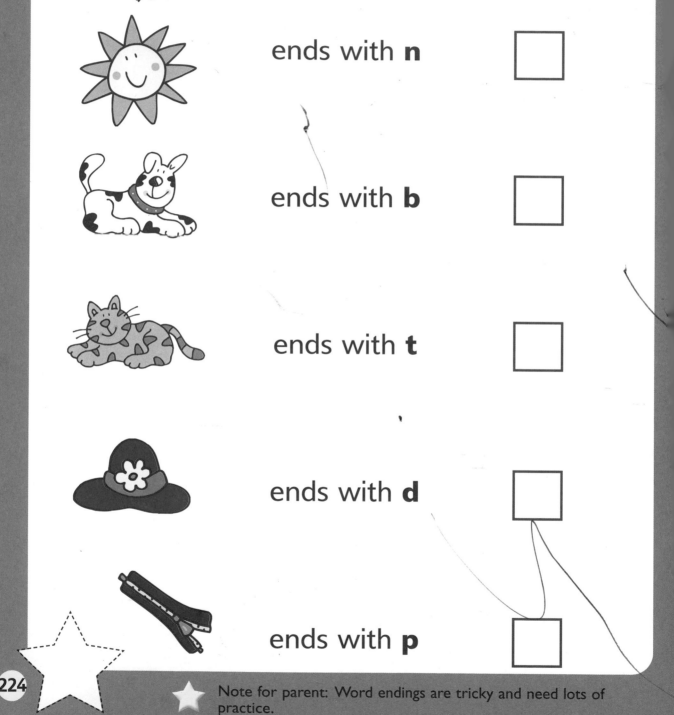

ends with **n** ☐

ends with **b** ☐

ends with **t** ☐

ends with **d** ☐

ends with **p** ☐

Note for parent: Word endings are tricky and need lots of practice.

Missing vowels

Trace the letters. Say the sounds.

a e i o u

Use the letters to finish these words.
Write them in.

c__t

p__g

n__t

d__g

b__s

Note for parent: Practise saying the vowel sounds with your child.

225

Fishing fun

These nets will only catch words with the right number of letters. Count the letters in each word and draw a line to join it to the right net.

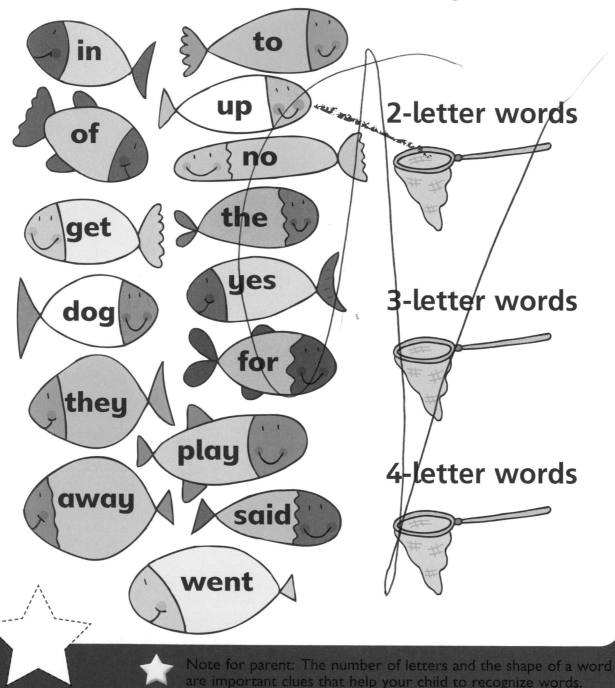

in

to

of

up

no

get

the

dog

yes

for

they

play

away

said

went

2-letter words

3-letter words

4-letter words

Note for parent: The number of letters and the shape of a word are important clues that help your child to recognize words.

I can read

Can you read and write all the words on this snail?

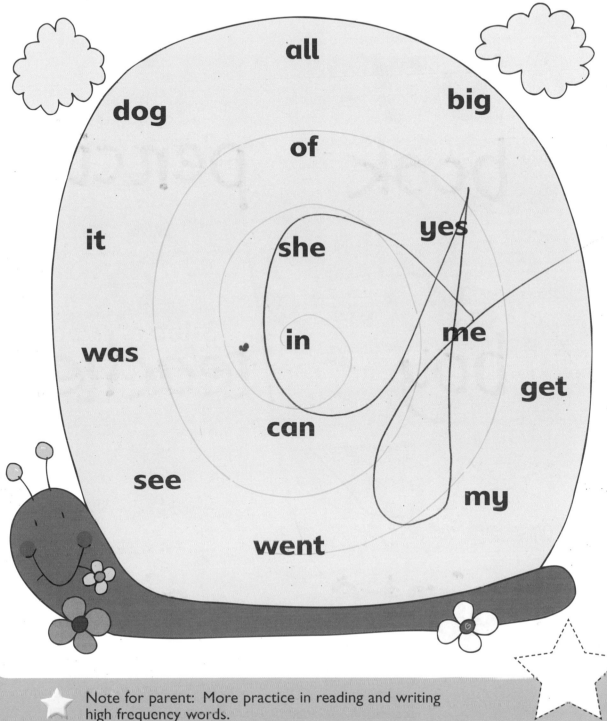

all

big

dog

of

it

yes

she

was

in

me

get

can

see

my

went

Note for parent: More practice in reading and writing high frequency words.

At school

Look at the pictures.
Trace the letters to write the words.
Read the words.

book

pencil

boy

teacher

paints

girl

Note for parent: Remind your child to start each letter at the right point.

Today's homework

Write each word under the correct picture.

hat cat net dog bus pig mop sun

----------------   ----------------

----------------   ----------------

----------------   ----------------

----------------   ----------------

Word bank

Can you read these words? Tick each word as you read it.

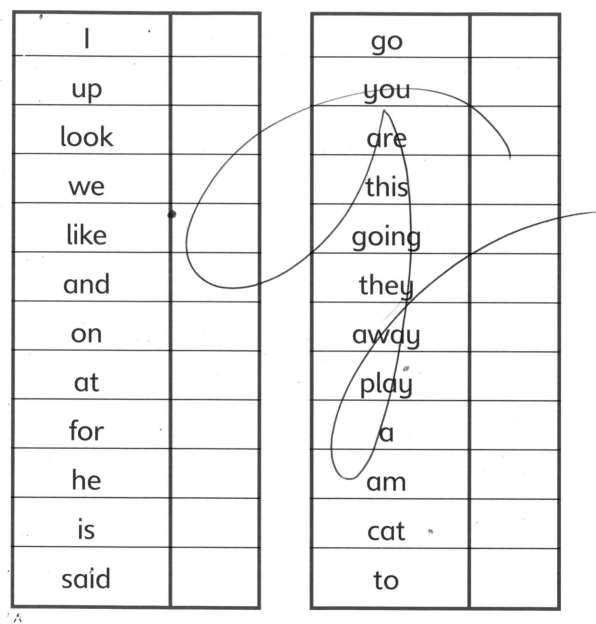

I		go	
up		you	
look		are	
we		this	
like		going	
and		they	
on		away	
at		play	
for		a	
he		am	
is		cat	
said		to	

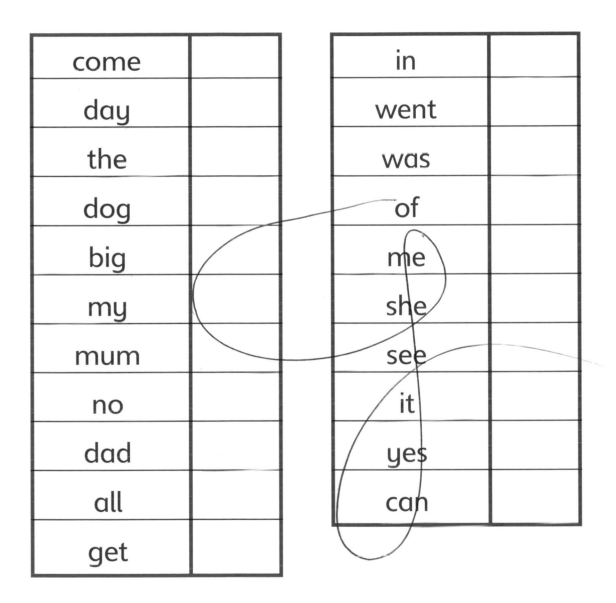

come		in	
day		went	
the		was	
dog		of	
big		me	
my		she	
mum		see	
no		it	
dad		yes	
all		can	
get			

Note for parent: Not all children will read at the same age. Always give your child lots of praise and encouragement.

Answers

Page 10

Page 11

Page 12 | in | on | under |

Page 14
The red snake is shortest.
The green snake is longest.

Page 15

Page 16
The elephant and the tractor are heavy.

Page 17

Pages 18–19

Page 20
There are 2 houses.
There are 3 flags.

Page 21

The number 2 is missing.

Page 23
1 horse, 2 dogs, 3 cats,
4 rabbits, 5 ducks.

Page 24
The blue circle is the smallest.
The purple circle is the biggest.

Page 28

Page 30
yellow square,
blue circle,
green triangle.

Page 31

Page 32

Page 33

Page 34

There are 5 candles on the cake.

Page 35

Page 36

Page 38
1 ship, 2 buckets, 3 spades, 4 hats,
5 shells, 6 starfish

Page 39

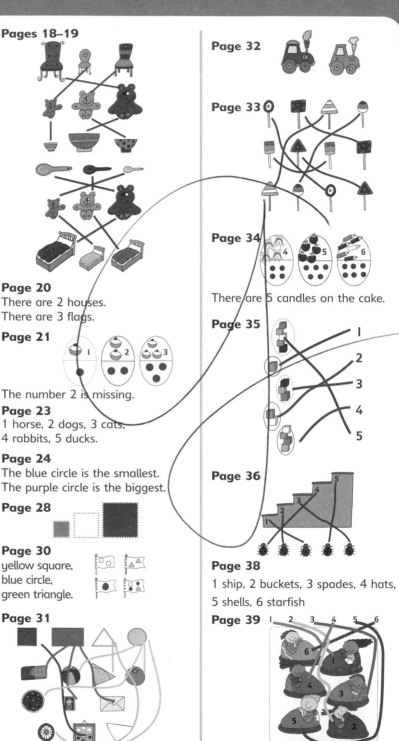

Answers

Page 41

Page 42

Page 45
10 bottles and 10 toes

Page 46

Page 47

1 2 3 4 5 6 7 8 9 10

Page 51

Pages 52–53

Page 59

Page 61

Page 64
Duck begins with the letter d.

Page 65
horse, bee, pig.

Page 66

begins with r ☑

begins with m ✗

begins with n ✗

Page 68
Kite begins with the letter k.

Page 69

f / ✗   j / ✗

Page 71

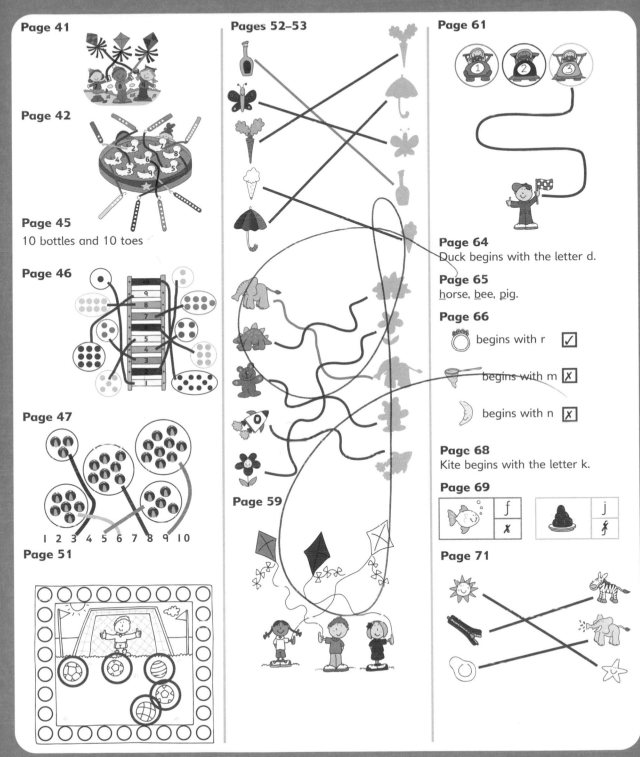

Answers

Page 74

Page 75

Page 76
queen, balloon, fish, dog, pig, yo-yo

Page 77

Page 81

Page 82

Page 85

Page 86
These people have more:

Page 89
1+1=2
1+1=2

Page 93
more holes ✓   more dogs ✓

Pages 94–95
2 flags
3 apples
4 butterflies
5 hats

Page 98
3 shells
4 balls
4 presents

Page 100
4 boats
4 trees

Page 102
5 stars
5 cars

Page 104

Page 105

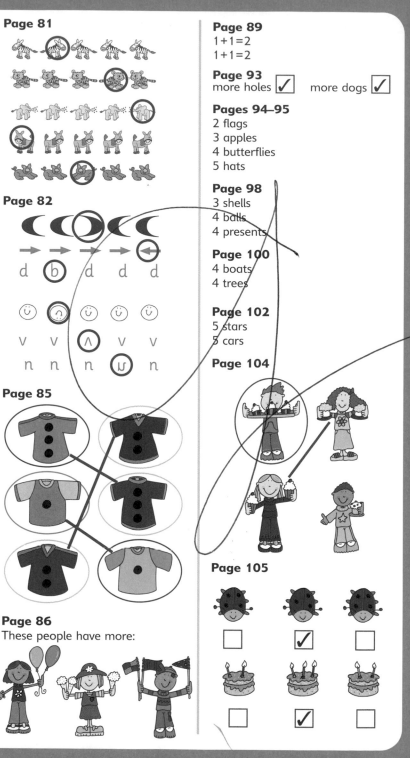

Answers

Pages 106–107

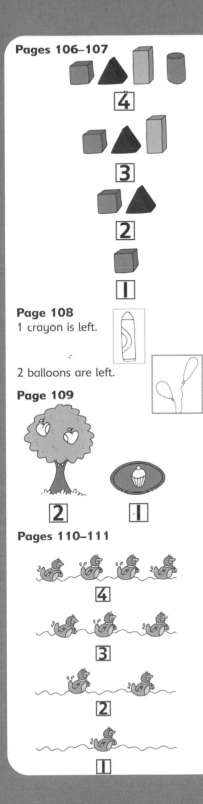

Page 108
1 crayon is left.

2 balloons are left.

Page 109

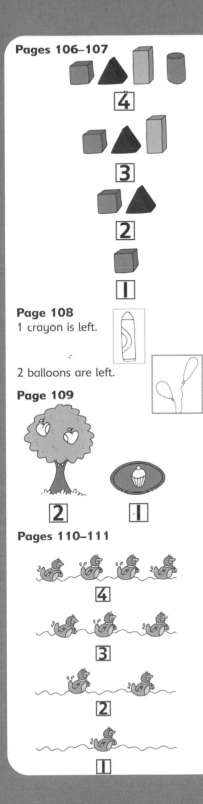

Pages 110–111

Page 112
1 apple, 3 oranges, 4 pears,
2 bananas

Page 113
6 take away 3 leaves 3
5 take away 3 leaves 2
9 take away 3 leaves 6
7 take away 3 leaves 4

Page 116
6 – 4 = 2
5 – 4 = 1
8 – 4 = 4
7 – 4 = 3

Page 117
9 – 4 = 5
10 – 4 = 6
4 – 4 = 0

Page 118
10 take away 5 leaves 5
8 take away 5 leaves 3
7 take away 5 leaves 2
9 take away 5 leaves 4

Page 119
10 – 5 = 5
6 – 5 = 1
9 – 5 = 4
5 – 5 = 0

Pages 122–123

Pages 124–125

Page 128
Possible answers are: d – dog, b –
ball, h – horse, k – kite, c – cake,
a – apple, s – sandwich, f – fox.

Page 129
man ring pig egg gate log

Page 132
Possible answers are: n – nest,
z – zebra, t – tiger, f – fox,
w – window, o – owl,
v – vase, k – kangaroo.

Page 133
a = apple, astronaut; b = boat,
ball; c = car, cat; d = duck, dog.
A F H W P B E

Page 134
tree: triangle, train, tractor.
bridge: brush, bread, bricks.
flag: flipper, fly, flower.

Page 135
fish, bird, hat, king, tent, zebra.

Page 136
hook/book, dog/frog, man/fan,
moon/spoon, bee/tree.

Page 137
spider: spaghetti, spoon, spade.
whale: wheelbarrow,
whistle, wheel.
sheep: shoe, shark, shell.

Page 138
dice, baby, dog, door,
ball, book, duck, bed.

Answers

Page 139
clock/cloud/clown;
dress/dragon/drum;
green/grass/grapes.

Page 140

Page 141
hats, socks, bats, balls, trees, stars.

Page 142
bed, dog, sun, book, tent, bus.

Page 143

Page 144
ambojsrwcl – owl, bcmsrotton –
moon, azcmsogkwy – cow,
endyrarnum – drum.

Page 145
hook/book, dog/frog, man/fan
book does not belong
bed, dog

Pages 146–147

Page 148

Page 149

Page 150
hat, bed, cup, pig, sun, box

Page 151

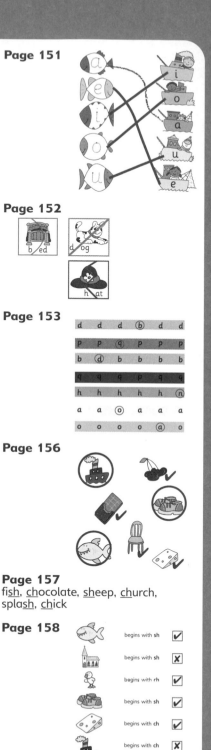

Page 152

Page 153

Page 156

Page 157
fish, chocolate, sheep, church,
splash, chick

Page 158

Answers

Page 159

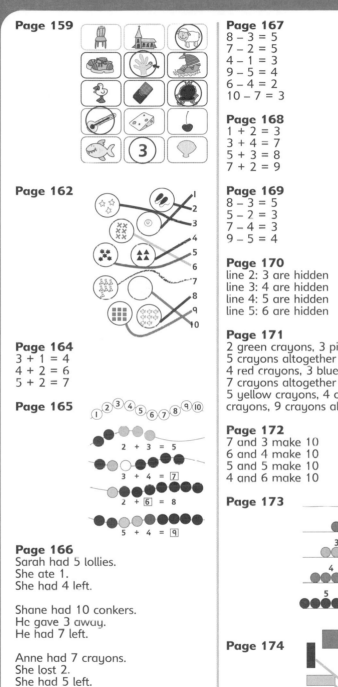

Page 162

Page 164
3 + 1 = 4
4 + 2 = 6
5 + 2 = 7

Page 165

Page 166
Sarah had 5 lollies.
She ate 1.
She had 4 left.

Shane had 10 conkers.
He gave 3 away.
He had 7 left.

Anne had 7 crayons.
She lost 2.
She had 5 left.

Ben had 8 cherries.
He ate 4.
He had 4 left.

Page 167
8 – 3 = 5
7 – 2 = 5
4 – 1 = 3
9 – 5 = 4
6 – 4 = 2
10 – 7 = 3

Page 168
1 + 2 = 3
3 + 4 = 7
5 + 3 = 8
7 + 2 = 9

Page 169
8 – 3 = 5
5 – 2 = 3
7 – 4 = 3
9 – 5 = 4

Page 170
line 2: 3 are hidden
line 3: 4 are hidden
line 4: 5 are hidden
line 5: 6 are hidden

Page 171
2 green crayons, 3 pink crayons,
5 crayons altogether
4 red crayons, 3 blue crayons,
7 crayons altogether
5 yellow crayons, 4 orange
crayons, 9 crayons altogether

Page 172
7 and 3 make 10
6 and 4 make 10
5 and 5 make 10
4 and 6 make 10

Page 173

Page 174

Page 175

Page 176

Page 177

Page 178

Page 179

Page 181

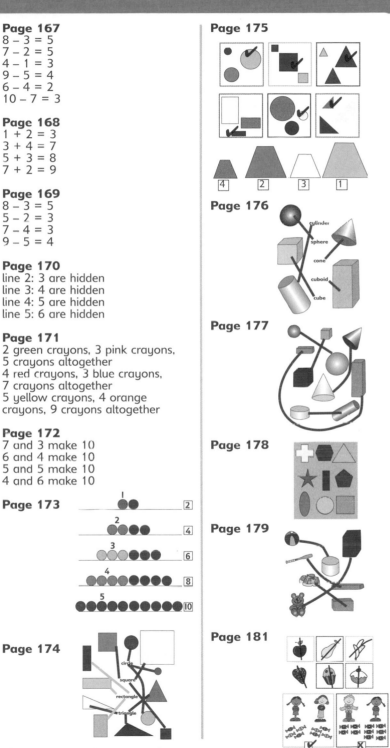

Answers

Page 182

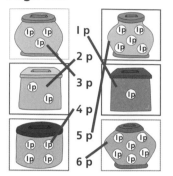

1 p
2 p
3 p
4 p
5 p
6 p

Page 183
Basket 1: 6p
Basket 2: 7p
Basket 3: 8p

Page 184
2p and 2p makes 4p
3p and 3p makes 6p
4p and 4p makes 8p
5p and 5p makes 10p

Page 187

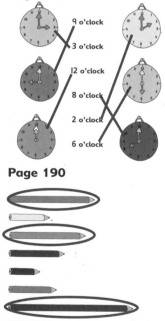

9 o'clock
3 o'clock
12 o'clock
8 o'clock
2 o'clock
6 o'clock

Page 190

The longest pencil is purple.
The shortest pencil is light red.

Page 191

Page 192

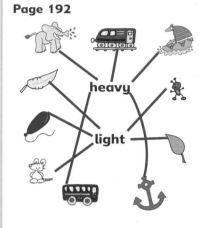

heavy

light

Page 193

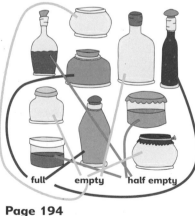

full   empty   half empty

Page 194
Line 2: 3 and 7
Line 3: 5 and 5
Line 4: 1 and 9
Line 5: 6 and 4
Line 6: 3 and 7

Page 195

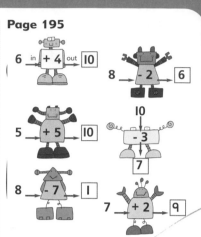

6 in + 4 out 10
8 - 2 6
5 + 5 10
10 - 3 7
8 - 7 1
7 + 2 9

Pages 196–197

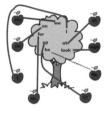

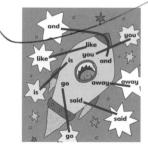

and
like
like
is
go
you
you
and
away
away
said
said
go

Page 199

Ben
Sam
Jo
Joshua
Ann
Jo
Ann
Ben
Sam
Joshua

238

Answers

Page 201

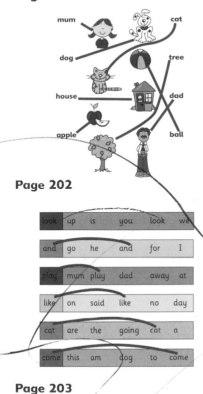

mum, cat, dog, tree, house, dad, apple, ball

Page 202

look	up	is	you	look	we
and	go	he	and	for	I
play	mum	play	dad	away	at
like	on	said	like	no	day
cat	are	the	going	cat	a
come	this	am	dog	to	come

Page 203

dog, mum, dog, dad, pig, mum, cat, pig, dad, sun, cat, sun

Page 204

<u>d</u>og, <u>m</u>um, cat, <u>d</u>ad, <u>p</u>ig, egg, <u>h</u>at, <u>l</u>og

Page 205

dad, ~~apple~~, dog, mum, ~~net~~, mouse, ball, ~~door~~, bed, cat, car, ~~sun~~, house, hat, ~~you~~

Page 206

cat/hat, net/pen, pig/zip, dog/fox, sun/bus

Page 207

1 letter – a, I
2 letters – on, at, up, is, go, we, he, am, no
3 letters – for, you, and,
4 letters – like, look, away, said,

Page 208

Page 209

cat, pen, fan, dog, mum, dad, pig, cup

Page 211

house, roof, window, door, garage

Page 212

dog, ca<u>t</u>, mu<u>m</u>, da<u>d</u>, bu<u>s</u>, car

Page 213

This is my <u>cat</u>.
It <u>is</u> white.
It has <u>a</u> long tail.
This is a <u>dog</u>.
It <u>can</u> bark.
It is <u>big</u>.

Page 217

<u>sh</u>eep, <u>sh</u>oes, <u>ch</u>urch, <u>ch</u>air

Page 218

<u>th</u>umb, <u>th</u>ree, <u>t</u>ooth, ba<u>th</u>, <u>th</u>ermometer, <u>th</u>rone

Page 219

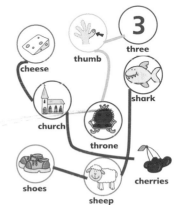

cheese, thumb, three, shark, church, throne, shoes, sheep, cherries

Page 220

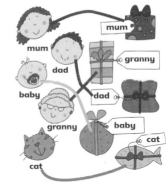

mum, granny, dad, dad, baby, granny, baby, cat, cat

Pages 222

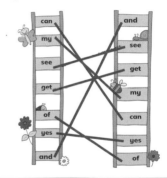

can, and, my, see, see, get, get, my, of, can, yes, yes, and, of

Answers

Page 223

Page 224

ends with n ✔

ends with b ✘

ends with t ✔

ends with d ✘

ends with p ✔

Page 225
cat, pig, net, dog, bus

Page 226
2-letter words – in, to, of, up, no,
3-letter words – get, the, yes,
dog, for
4-letter words– they, play, said,
went, away

Page 229
hat, cat, dog, net, bus, pig, sun,
mop